GETTING IT RIGHT FOR YOUNG CHILDREN FROM DIVERSE BACKGROUNDS

APPLYING RESEARCH TO IMPROVE PRACTICE

Linda M. Espinosa

Washington, DC

Learning Solutions

New York   Boston   San Francisco
London   Toronto   Sydney   Tokyo   Singapore   Madrid
Mexico City   Munich   Paris   Cape Town   Hong Kong   Montreal

Taken from: Courtesy of Photodisc/Getty Images.

Getting It Right for Young Children from Diverse Backgrounds:
Applying Research to Improve Practice
by Linda M. Espinosa
Copyright © 2010 by Pearson Education, Inc.
Published by Prentice Hall
Upper Saddle River, New Jersey 07458

This special edition published in cooperation with Pearson Learning Solutions.

Pearson Learning Solutions, 501 Boylston Street, Suite 900, Boston, MA 02116
A Pearson Education Company
www.pearsoned.com

naeyc
Copublished by
National Association for the Education of Young Children
1313 L Street NW, Suite 500
Washington, DC 20005-4101
www.naeyc.org

NAEYC Item #793

Printed in the United States of America

1 2 3 4 5 6 7 8 9 10 V312 14 13 12 11 10

2009220254

RG

ISBN 10: 0-558-57017-8
ISBN 13: 978-0-558-57017-0

PREFACE

This book is the product of more than 30 years' work with young children and families from very diverse backgrounds. I have worked as a practitioner and a researcher, an administrator and a policy maker, a trainer and an evaluator, as well as a consultant to many school districts, state departments of education, and educational foundations to help identify and promote effective practices and policies for young children who often have no one to speak for them. My own personal history also includes being raised in a large Hispanic family that experienced many of the conditions described in this book. In fact, what I witnessed as a child from a non-mainstream home growing up in 1950s and 1960s America combined with my professional experiences and knowledge has fueled my sense of urgency about the messages in this book.

As a practitioner, I have personally witnessed what a difference hopeful attitudes, well-informed outreach, skilled instruction, and well-supported teachers can make for children and families who are often stressed beyond their limits with the daily demands of meeting their basic needs. I have participated in well-crafted early education programs, staffed by qualified and caring educators who successfully partnered with families speaking no English, to joyfully educate young children and prepare them for the rigors of formal academic instruction. More recently, as a researcher, I have conducted empirical studies, published research, and synthesized the academic literature on effective preschool approaches for young children who have been deemed "at risk" for school failure. I have also conducted hundreds of professional development sessions for early childhood practitioners who are eager for well-researched strategies they can take home and try out next week. This has convinced me that there is a need to translate the scientific evidence into practical guidance so that teachers will have the knowledge and confidence to implement effective practices.

Unfortunately, I have also seen firsthand the consequences of inadequate training, misguided practices, neglect, misunderstanding, and even outright bigotry on the life forces of bright, curious, and highly verbal children who had the misfortune to be born into poverty or faced the challenge of learning English in addition to their home language during the preschool years. I have seen firsthand how children's inherent *eagerness to learn* and participate in a social community, their youthful quirkiness and delight in the mysteries of the world, can all be muted before they ever begin formal schooling. This book offers prospective teachers, practitioners, trainers, and professional educators a perspective that represents my accumulated knowledge combined with the available scientific evidence; it is grounded in real-life experiences and guided by current rigorous research findings.

My intent is to sort through and synthesize the latest scientific evidence on development and school achievement for young children who have historically struggled with the demands of schooling; this knowledge base is then combined with my own experiences in inner city schools as an administrator and evaluator to offer classroom and program recommendations. Throughout my career in early childhood education, I have felt a sense of urgency about improving the conditions of schooling for children and families, particularly those who are from nontraditional backgrounds, those who speak a language other than English, and those who face the challenges of poverty. Because of my own background and professional expertise,

I have focused this book on the successful education of children from linguistically and culturally diverse backgrounds and those who are growing up in poverty.

It is critically important that *all* children in this country receive high-quality education that provides them with the tools to successfully navigate the currents of adulthood. Early childhood education has the potential to improve the life chances of all young children and is being touted as an answer to the stubborn reality of educational inequities. As we move forward on the early childhood agenda, it is important that we *GET IT RIGHT.* I believe that we now *know* enough to successfully educate *all* children; it is now a question of translating this knowledge to specific strategies and practices. It is incumbent on researchers and policy experts to make this information accessible to *all* teachers.

ORGANIZATION OF CHAPTERS

Chapter 1 outlines the converging social and educational conditions that have prompted this book. It also contains a vignette that illustrates what can occur to one child, "Warren," when schools and teachers are not adequately prepared to meet the range of diverse needs present in today's children and families. The importance of high-quality early childhood in addressing educational inequities is discussed in Chapter 1.

In Chapter 2, I profile the demographic characteristics of the current and future population of young children entering early childhood programs. Immigration patterns, fertility rates, and workforce participation are all contributing to a larger, more diverse prekindergarten and primary grade population. For example, the National Center of Education Statistics (NCES), the National Institute for Early Educational Research (NIEER), and several recent government reports all underscore the dramatic increase in the number of children ages 3 to 5 who are cared for in an out-of-home setting. For the first time in U.S. history, the majority of our young children receive their early care and education from a paid provider, not a family member. A growing percentage of these children speak a language other than English at home and are from diverse cultures; many are also growing up in impoverished home environments. I examine these trends and the range of early childhood programs currently available. I also discuss the influence of the educational standards movement on early childhood education practices.

The scientific evidence reviewed in Chapter 3 indicates new understandings of young children's early intellectual capabilities and the role of enriched early learning environments and positive, nurturing relationships. The substantial impact of the environment on the child's rate and level of development suggests the potential for early childhood programs to impact children's development, school readiness, and lifelong learning. We know that development is a function of both genetic potential and the interactions and experiences early in life that shape the architecture of the brain. Chapter 3 summarizes scientific research from multiple disciplines that should be used to guide informed early childhood policies and practices.

In Chapter 4, I discuss the conditions of early learning that affect children living in poverty. The literature about resiliency and what early childhood programs can do to promote resiliency in children living in economically disadvantaged circumstances is reviewed. It also offers early childhood programs guidance on how to design practices that will enhance the personal resilience of young vulnerable children. Specific teaching strategies that have been shown to be effective for children who are facing difficult early challenges are described. In addition, methods for reaching out to families who are struggling economically are suggested.

Chapter 5 focuses on the research that helps us understand how young children who are English language learners develop, how having two languages influences overall development, and the effectiveness of different curricula and program approaches for this group of children. Six common myths about English language learners are described and challenged by current research findings. The process of learning a second language during the early childhood years, the factors that influence the rate of English acquisition, and the consequences of home language loss are all addressed in this chapter. Chapter 5 also outlines the features of preschool programs and specific teaching strategies that have been shown to promote positive outcomes for children from culturally and linguistically diverse backgrounds.

In Chapter 6, I describe in detail many specific teaching strategies based on the research summarized in Chapter 5. The importance of establishing agreed-upon program goals for language development and implementing a comprehensive curriculum are discussed. Dozens of specific teaching strategies that all teachers can apply are presented along with specific recommendations for how to assess the progress of English language learners.

Finally, Chapter 7 describes the resources and policies that will be needed to systematically improve our practices to achieve the vision recommended in this book. To create a stable, sustainable, and effective system we will need to do the following: (1) bolster our national will, (2) continuously improve and incorporate rigorous research, (3) link early childhood to national educational policies, and (4) advocate for sufficient resources to achieve substantial progress for *all* children.

This book is dedicated to the children and families who have overcome obstacles to get their children to an early childhood program and depend on us to have current knowledge and skills; it is also dedicated to the teachers who show the courage and dedication to show up every day and work on behalf of young children who need our best teachers and brightest ideas.

To make this book more useful to practitioners, real-life scenarios are presented throughout each chapter; specific curricular approaches are described whenever possible, and a list of relevant resources is provided. It is my hope to educate, to inspire, and to sufficiently raise the level of concern so as to prevent any future "Warren" stories.

ACKNOWLEDGMENTS

This book, and in fact all of my work, is possible because of the enduring support, patience, and affection of my husband, James Laffey. His patient, calming influence, and optimistic approach toward life has kept me focused on the big picture. I also want to thank my daughter, Andrea Laffey, who assisted with many editorial tasks that helped me enormously. I must thank my editor, Julie Peters, who has prodded, inspired, and nagged me at every step of this journey.

Finally, I would like to thank the following reviewers for their feedback: Patricia Cantor, Plymouth State University; Gina Cicco, Hostos Community College, The City University of New York; Stephanie Deering, South Plains College; Shaquam Urquhart Edwards, College of Marin; Hersh C. Waxman, Texas A&M University; and Marlene Zepeda, California State University, Los Angeles.

—*Linda M. Espinosa*

ABOUT THE AUTHOR

 **Dr. Linda M. Espinosa,** Professor of Early Childhood Education (Ret.) at the University of Missouri, Columbia, has served as the Co-Director of the National Institute for Early Education Research (NIEER) at Rutgers University and Vice President of Education at Bright Horizons Family Solutions. Her recent research and policy work has focused on effective curriculum and assessment practices for young children from low-income families who are dual language learners. She currently serves as the Co-Chair of the First Five Los Angeles County Universal Preschool Research Advisory Committee and is a member of the National Task Force on Early Childhood Education for Hispanics Technical Advisory Group. Dr. Espinosa also served on the Head Start National Reporting System (NRS) Technical Advisory Group.

Dr. Espinosa has worked extensively with low-income Hispanic/Latino children and families throughout the state of California as a school administrator and program director in San Francisco, San Jose, and Redwood City. She developed and directed the Family Focus for School Success program in Redwood City, California, which has received state and national recognition. She has published more than 50 research articles, book chapters, and training manuals on how to establish effective educational services for low-income, minority families and children who are acquiring English as a second language. More recently, she has lectured and consulted widely both nationally (California, Oklahoma, Illinois, New Jersey, Colorado, Washington, New York, North Carolina, Nebraska, New Mexico, Washington, DC) and internationally (China, Canada, Australia, New Zealand).

Dr. Espinosa is the past treasurer of the National Association for the Education of Young Children (NAEYC) Governing Board and participated on the National Academy of Sciences Research Roundtable on Head Start. She has recently completed a secondary analysis of the Early Childhood Longitudinal Study—Kindergarten Cohort (ECLS-K) on the school achievement patterns of language minority children. Dr. Espinosa also was a member of the National Academy of Sciences, National Research Board Committee on Early Childhood Pedagogy project and a contributing author to *Eager to Learn: Educating Our Preschoolers,* published by the National Academies of Science. She completed her B.A. at the University of Washington, her Ed.M. at Harvard University, and her Ph.D. in Educational Psychology at the University of Chicago.

BRIEF CONTENTS

CONTENTS

Appendices

Early Childhood Education, Diversity, and Educational Equity

Whether or not children will be successful students depends greatly on the quality of their experiences in early childhood.

U.S. DEPARTMENT OF HEALTH AND HUMAN SERVICES, 2003

In the last decade, early childhood education has been promoted as a remedy for many aspects of educational inequity; it has been associated with increased academic achievement and school completion, reduced special education placement, teenage pregnancy, welfare dependence, and incarceration rates for children from minority and low-income backgrounds (Gormley, Gayer, Phillips, & Dawson, 2005; Isaacs, 2008; Magnuson, Ruhm, & Walgfogel, 2007; Schweinhart et al., 2005). With more U.S. children born into poverty, single-parent homes, non-English-speaking families, and unstable social conditions, together with a higher premium for educational success, the stakes for success and failure have become higher for individual children as well as social institutions. Our schools and social service agencies are under enormous pressure to show concrete outcomes and benefits for the children and families they serve. The following factors have converged to create a set of conditions that has elevated the issues of early childhood education to the forefront of our national educational agenda:

- The preschool population has become highly diverse culturally, ethnically, linguistically, and economically.
- Greater percentages of young children from all social and economic backgrounds are cared for outside the home and family.

- There is overwhelming, credible scientific evidence for the enduring educational and economic benefits of enriched preschool programs.
- There is compelling new research from neuroscientists, biologists, psychologists, and educators about the intellectual and social capabilities of infants and young children.
- The elements of high-quality preschool have been carefully designed and researched; effective teaching practices that promote long-term literacy and school success can be articulated.
- There is a significant and persistent academic achievement gap between low-income children from diverse backgrounds and their more affluent White peers; much of this test score gap is evident at kindergarten entry. High-quality early education can reduce this gap prior to school entry.
- The early childhood teaching force is threatened by inadequate preparation, low compensation, and rapid turnover.

Together, these conditions call for a renewed and sustained effort to ensure high-quality early learning opportunities for our youngest and most vulnerable students.

Consider the following scenario based on an actual event supervised by the author:

As he strode into the computer lab, Warren (pseudonym), a 5-year-old kindergarten student, managed to touch every object in his path—three VCRs, two tables, two computers, and several chairs, some of which he pounded with his palm. He was headed for the third computer on the left, which had been set up for him with specially selected math software. When the assistant asked him if he needed help getting started, he mumbled "no," and eagerly placed his hand over the mouse and began to respond to the directions on the computer. For the next 23 minutes, Warren declined any assistance, preferring to correct his errors through trial and error. He was intently focused on the computer screen, sometimes smiling, occasionally talking to himself about what he was doing, but intently grabbing the geometric shapes with the cursor, moving them into their designated spots to form complex geometric designs—a skill that takes considerable focus and fine motor control—and grinning triumphantly when the new designs were completed.

After his computer session, I interviewed Warren about his experiences, feelings, and attitude towards the computer and school in general. He reported that he liked doing the "games" on the computer because he was good at it. When asked about school in general, he replied, "I hate school. Everyone hates me because I'm bad." He also said he hated his teacher because she called him "bad." When Warren expressed his feelings about school, his face was glum, he stared at the ground, and his whole body appeared rigid.

I followed Warren back to his kindergarten classroom to report his accomplishments to his teacher and observe how he transitioned into the routine of classroom life. The class was watching a large video projection of a phonics software lesson that required repeating the sounds and naming initial consonants. Warren stiffly walked to his desk that had been placed against the far wall, some distance from the other children who were at tables and from the teacher. He sat down for about 10 seconds, never even glanced at the screen, and then jumped up and proceeded to pinch a young boy on the back and grab his papers. The teacher responded by sternly saying to Warren, "Get back in your seat and stop bothering the other children." This sent Warren back to his desk, where he stayed for about 20 seconds before he was under his desk, making distracting noises and getting into trouble again.

I was describing what a great job Warren was doing with his computer time, how he was concentrating for over 20 minutes at a time and was intent on learning the math lessons independently, when the teacher interrupted and said, "Warren just can't control himself. He is always in trouble, and we are planning on putting him on medication."

Clearly, this young boy has educational, social, emotional, and possibly medical needs that most likely will not be met in his current kindergarten program. Warren has initiative, eagerness, and cognitive abilities, but he also has vulnerabilities that make it difficult for him to succeed within a traditional teacher-directed classroom. The kindergarten teacher has had minimal preparation or training in early childhood and no specialized preparation for working with children from diverse backgrounds. She has a large class of 25 children, all African American children from low-income homes, has no assistant, and is expected to meet the district academic standards by May. She has received limited district in-service education focused on the district achievement benchmarks and a skills-based early reading program that has carefully scripted lessons for the teachers to follow.

Warren is being raised by a mother who did not complete her high school education, is on public assistance, and was recently released from a drug treatment program. Neither Warren nor the teacher has been adequately prepared to be successful under these conditions.

In this book I will outline an agenda for the future that synthesizes the most recent information about the educational needs of children ages 3 to 6 and recommends practices that promote learning for *all* young children with an emphasis on children who are not native English speakers, those who are growing up in poverty, and children who have diverse cultural backgrounds. No child should have to face the bleak educational future that Warren faces, and no early childhood teacher should have to face these working conditions without support, resources, and adequate preparation and training. Unfortunately, too many of our young children and their teachers are poorly prepared to meet the academic demands of early schooling. The costs to society are enormous, such as illiteracy, school dropouts, juvenile delinquency, welfare dependency, and criminal behaviors. However, the costs to the individual children and their families are even more ruinous: unfulfilled lives and unrealized potential, stunted intellectual and emotional development, and decreased capacity to fully participate in the American Dream.

THE WHY OF EARLY CHILDHOOD EDUCATION

Brain research over the last few decades has contributed important knowledge about how specific learning experiences during the first years of life help to shape the neural circuitry of the growing brain. Scientists have been able to document the rapid growth of brain development based on enriched learning opportunities that allow young children to make connections across different regions of the brain, process language, develop cognitive abilities, and process emotions—in effect, to think, develop ideas, and become socialized into their worlds (National Scientific Council on the Developing Child at Harvard University, 2007c). This research by neuroscientists, biologists, and psychologists affirms what developmental, psychological, and educational research has documented over many years: that the foundations for school and life success are established during a child's earliest years.

It has been well established that high-quality early education is a cost-effective method of improving the long-term educational and social outcomes for children living in poverty. Educational research has consistently found that high-quality preschool programs enhance children's school readiness, contribute to long-term academic success, and are cost-effective (Barnett, 2008; Reynolds, Temple, Robertson, & Mann, 2001).

> "[T]he findings tell the same story—that those most at risk will make the greatest gains from early childhood programs (and conversely the social costs will be the highest for a failure to intervene on their behalf)" (Galinsky, 2006, p. 3).

When young children from impoverished homes have the opportunity to attend early childhood programs that are of high quality, they are better prepared for the demands of formal schooling and they are much more likely to finish high school. Many studies have also found that children from low-income households and children who are at risk for school failure benefit the most from these programs. In fact, one researcher recently summed up the research by stating "the findings tell the same story—that those most at risk will make the greatest gains from early childhood programs (and conversely the social costs will be the highest for a failure to intervene on their behalf)" (Galinsky, 2006, p. 3).

Creating the right conditions for learning and positive development during the preschool years is much more likely to be effective and less costly than waiting to address learning problems that occur later in a child's life. The neuroscientists describe this process as "wiring the circuitry of the brain" correctly from the earliest age through enriched cognitive and social learning opportunities. Early rigorous evaluations of model early childhood programs for 3- and 4-year-olds living in poverty have shown returns on each public dollar invested as high as 17:1, with average annual return rates of 18% over 35 years (Heckman & Masterov, 2007). This research demonstrates that investing in expanded early learning opportunities will yield positive economic outcomes as a result of improved child functioning. That is why many leading economists are advocating for larger investments in quality early education as one of the best public investments and one of the few proven routes to improved social functioning. Many of our chronic social problems like high school dropout rates for low-income children, adult unemployment and welfare dependence, and juvenile criminal behavior have been shown to be positively affected by high-quality early childhood interventions (Isaacs, 2008; Reynolds et al., 2001; Schweinhart et al., 2005).

WHY THE INCREASED FOCUS ON EARLY CHILDHOOD PROGRAMS RIGHT NOW?

Children, families, and schools are under enormous pressure to achieve higher standards based on the No Child Left Behind Act. There is a significant and enduring achievement gap between middle-class children and low-income children, particularly low-income children of color. Recent analyses based on large national studies suggest that much of this academic achievement gap is evident at kindergarten entry (Hart & Risley, 1995, 1999; Lee & Burkam, 2002). This achievement gap between different groups of children is difficult and becomes increasingly more difficult and costly even for highly skilled, more experienced teachers to address as children get older (Education Trust, 2003a, 2003b). Many researchers, educators, and policy makers view early education as an opportunity to equalize educational opportunities and decrease the achievement gap between low- and high-income children (Barnett, 2002; Schweinhart et al., 2005). Therefore, we have seen a steady increase in state and locally funded preschool programs, with a few states legislating voluntary preschool for all 4-year-old children (e.g., Florida, Oklahoma, Georgia, and New York).

Although the general trend is toward greater investments in early childhood education across the states, the range of funding levels, access, and durability varies significantly. Some states provide programs for all preschool children living in low-income communities and fund at high levels (e.g., New Jersey's Abbott districts funded at almost $11,000 per child enrolled in 2008). Other states fund prekindergarten efforts at much more modest levels, with two states spending less than $2,000 per child enrolled (Barnett, Epstein, Friedman, Boyd, & Hustedt, 2008). Most states use a combination of federal, state, and local funding to provide targeted early learning opportunities for children who meet certain eligibility requirements. Children from the lowest income homes and those who are learning English as a second language typically have the highest priority for these early educational services.

In our zeal to improve educational opportunities and outcomes for children vulnerable to school failure, it is critical that we *get it right*. It will do no good to have many thousands of young children spend their days in well-intended but poorly designed and ill-equipped early learning settings. We now have sufficient, rigorous research from multiple disciplines that presents a compelling case for both the long-term benefits of effective early educational services as well as the features of these programs that make them effective. This book represents my analysis of the research on best practices and my reflections on more than 30 years of professional experiences with how to meet the needs of young, vulnerable children who deserve to be well educated, nurtured, and respected.

> We now have sufficient, rigorous research from multiple disciplines that presents a compelling case for both the long-term benefits of effective early educational services as well as the features of these programs that make them effective.

PUBLIC PROGRAMS FOR YOUNG CHILDREN

One by-product of our increased knowledge about the effectiveness of early education has been heightened attention to the design, funding, and evaluation of early childhood education programs in most state departments of education. In fact, 46 states in 2006 had legislation that supported some public funding for preschool programs (Education Commission of the States, 2006). These publicly funded programs range from Universal Prekindergarten (UPK), which is offered in

Increasingly, preschool-aged children are attending center-based educational programs.

three states (Florida, Georgia, and Oklahoma), to voluntary half-day programs offered at the school district's discretion. UPK programs typically are provided in local communities to all eligible children who elect to enroll; they are funded through a combination of local, county, and state dollars. In California, although the state government does not fund UPK, many counties (e.g., Los Angeles, San Francisco, Santa Clara, and San Mateo) have decided to move forward and offer UPK themselves. California also passed a proposition that levies a 50-cent tax on each pack of cigarettes that has been used to create First 5 California, also known as the California Children and Families Commission. This commission funds education, health services, child care, and other early educational programs for California's children ages birth to 5. Across all states, the majority of children served in public early educational programs are 4 years of age, with 3-year-olds attending center-based programs at much lower rates (Barnett et al., 2008).

Funding for early childhood education can range from enhanced support for Head Start and/or child care to half-day school-year preschool programs. Although 46 states provide funding for some type of early childhood education, when we include only state-funded prekindergarten programs, the total number of states counted in 2008 dropped from 46 to 38 (Barnett et al., 2008). Twelve states provided no public funding for prekindergarten programs in 2008: Alaska, Hawaii, Idaho, Indiana, Mississippi, Montana, New Hampshire, North Dakota, Rhode Island, South Dakota, Utah, and Wyoming (Barnett et al., 2008). These states may offer some combination of federal, Head Start, or local funding for preschool programs, but they have no official state-funded prekindergarten program. Nevertheless, 2000 census data revealed that more than half (52%) of all children ages 3 to 5 who were not in kindergarten were enrolled in a public or privately funded preschool program (Lopez & de Cos, 2004).

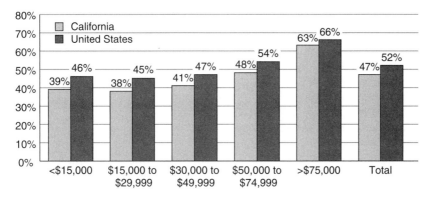

FIGURE 1.1 Preschool and nursery enrollment rates in California and the United States by family income, 2000 (children ages 3 to 5 not in kindergarten).

Note: California Research Bureau, California State Library, using the IPUMS 2000 (5% sample).

Source: From *Preschool and Childcare Enrollment in California* (No. CRB99009), by E. S. Lopez & P. L. de Cos, 2004, Sacramento, CA: California Research Bureau, p. 25.

More recently, the National Institute for Early Educational Research has determined that more than 80% of all 4-year-olds attend some type of preschool program, public or private (Barnett, et al., 2008). In 2000, this represented almost 5 million young children who were regularly being cared for and educated by adults outside of the home. These numbers continue to increase annually. Enrollment rates in both California and the United States vary by both race/ethnicity and family income levels (see Figures 1.1 and 1.2). Nationally, preschool children from families who earn less than $50,000 and Latino children are the least likely to be enrolled in any kind of a nursery or preschool program.

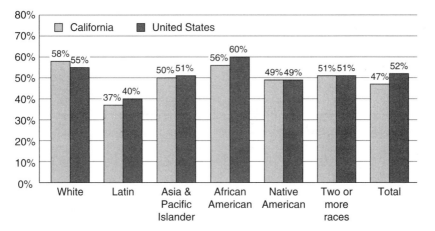

FIGURE 1.2 Preschool and nursery enrollment rates in California and the United States, 2000 (children ages 3 to 5 not in kindergarten).

Note: California Research Bureau, California State Library, using the IPUMS 2000 (5% sample).

Source: From *Preschool and Childcare Enrollment in California* (No. CRB99009), by E. S. Lopez & P. L. de Cos, 2004, Sacramento, CA: California Research Bureau, p. 24.

Unfortunately, many of our most vulnerable children—those from low-income homes, those who do not speak English in the home, and those who have recently immigrated to the United States—are disproportionately not enrolled in any type of early education program (Barnett & Yarsiz, 2007). We are also finding that even when these children who stand to gain the most from early education do attend, the programs they attend are less likely to be judged as high quality (Karoly, Ghosh-Dastidar, Zellman, Perlman, & Fernyhough, 2008). For a more complete description of the status of early education nationally, current legislation and regulations, the range of program and funding options, attendance rates, exemplary practices and policies, and public opinion about early childhood education, see the National Institute for Early Education Research (NIEER) Web site at http://nieer.org.

Summary

Recent developments have converged to elevate early childhood education to the forefront of our educational agenda. Increasing diversity of our population of young children, combined with compelling new research about the critical role of early learning opportunities, call for a renewed and sustained public effort to ensure that *all* young children have access to high-quality early education.

Most states are increasing their investments in publicly funded programs for young children and are targeting children who are vulnerable to school failure, for example, those who are from low-income homes and those who do not speak English as their first language. At this juncture in educational growth, it is critical that we *get it right*. These investments need to be well spent. Children and families will not thrive and important benefits will not occur if many young children spend their days in well-intended but poorly designed, ineffective, and ill-equipped early learning settings.

We now have scientific research from multiple disciplines that presents a compelling case for both the long-term benefits of effective early educational services as well as the features of these programs that make them effective. This book represents my synthesis of the research on best practices and my reflections on more than 30 years of professional experiences with how to meet the needs of young, vulnerable children who deserve to be well educated, nurtured, and respected.

Reflection and Discussion Questions

1. What developments in your local community or nationally have you personally observed that indicate a heightened interest in early childhood education?
2. What kinds of differences do you think kindergarten teachers will notice between children who have experienced 2 years of high-quality preschool and those who have not had any preschool?
3. What types of programs and supports are available in your community for young children? What kinds of programs does your local school district provide for children ages birth to 5?

2

The Changing Face of Early Childhood in the United States

New Promises, New Pitfalls

Diverse voci fanno dolce note; cosi diversi scanni in nostra vita rendon dolce armonia.... [Diverse voices make sweet music; as diverse conditions in our life render sweet harmony....]

DANTE, *PARADISO* IV: 124–126

Throughout the United States, we are witnessing an expansion of the number of early childhood programs available as well as increased funding and public attention paid to the importance of early learning environments. There is growing recognition at all levels of society that the learning opportunities a child has before kindergarten are important for short-term and long-term benefits. We also have learned that the quality of early childhood experiences is critically important for children who do not have enriched home-learning opportunities. This knowledge gained over the past two decades has helped to fuel public support for the expansion of accessible, affordable, and high-quality preschool.

CURRENT DEMOGRAPHICS AND POPULATION PROJECTIONS

High quality early learning is like a "life jacket" for low-income kids. They need the life-preserver, whereas middle and upper-income kids already know how to swim and are not dependent on this to get ahead.

JEAN LAYZER, ABT ASSOCIATES, AS CITED IN KLEIN AND KNITZER, 2006

Just as our country has become more diverse linguistically, ethnically, and culturally, so has the population of children who attend early education and primary programs grown more diverse. Early education programs are now providing services to groups of children and families that have backgrounds, customs, languages, and pressures that are unfamiliar to teachers and staff. Although early childhood teachers are still predominantly White and female, children are increasingly from culturally and linguistically diverse and/or poverty households. To effectively meet the needs of all children and families, all early childhood practitioners will need to better understand the children they serve, their unique strengths, the conditions of their early learning environments, and how to effectively respond to their specific educational needs.

CHILDREN IN POVERTY

The number of young children growing up in poverty has been steadily increasing over the last decade. Between 2000 and 2005, the number increased by more than 11% (National Center for Children in Poverty, 2007). The Department of Health and Human Services (HHS) issues poverty guidelines in late January or early February of each year. These guidelines are based on federal estimates of the cost of food, shelter, clothing, and a limited amount of other needs for a family of two adults and two children. Developed more than 40 years ago, the official poverty measure is a specific dollar amount that varies by family size but is the same across the continental United States. In 2008 a family of four that earned less than $21,200 was considered *poor* while those who made between $21,200 and $42,000 were described as *low income*. In 2006, about 39% of all children in the United States— more than 28 million children—lived in poor or low-income families (National Center for Children in Poverty, 2007).

The census data also indicate that across the United States approximately 20% of all children under the age of 5 live in poverty (U.S. Census Bureau, 2003). This percentage increases dramatically for recent immigrant families, families that do not speak English, single-parent families, and those in certain geographical areas of the country.

Poverty is not equally distributed among the diverse groups in this country. It is more prevalent in southern states, with Mississippi having the highest official poverty rate: 27%. Overall, 18% of all children (13 million) live in poor families (those who earn less than $21,200/year), with 20% of children under 6 considered poor. Black, Latino, and American Indian children are more likely to live in poverty than their White counterparts. Almost 30% of Latino children live in poverty. That number is 35% for Black children and 29% for American Indian children, while it is 10% for White children (National Center for Children in Poverty, 2007). Immigrant families also tend to live below the poverty rate; in all states children of immigrant parents are

---

Avoid Stereotyping "The Poor"

There is great diversity among children and families who experience economic hardship. Research shows that many common perceptions about poor families are not accurate. About 40% of Americans will experience poverty at some point in their lives; only a small minority experience persistent and chronic poverty and family instability (National Center for Children in Poverty, 2007). In addition, more than 90% of low-income single mothers have only one, two, or three children. Most single mothers work hard and provide positive and nourishing environments for their children; achieving these goals with limited material resources is something to be celebrated.

A significant portion of families in America has experienced economic hardship, even if it is not lifelong. In America, poverty is most often not a permanent condition of families. In addition to the millions of families who struggle to make ends meet, millions of others are merely one health emergency, divorce, job loss, or other crisis away from financial devastation. In recent years, more and more families have become vulnerable to economic hardship.

---

more likely to live in poor families than children of native-born parents. The poverty rates for immigrant families range from 14% in New Jersey to 40% in Texas.

Children in these families face many economic hardships that often impede their ability to develop fully and reach their intellectual and physical potentials. Many low-income families are unable to provide adequate diets for their children, lack health insurance, live in inadequate housing in dangerous neighborhoods, and experience job instability (Douglas-Hall, Koball, & Chau, 2006). It is clear that poverty places many stressors on families that reduce their ability to provide the continuous nurturing, enhanced learning opportunities, and material resources necessary to promote optimal growth and development of their children. In addition, it is important not to stereotype children and families who are living in poverty (see box above).

These unequal learning opportunities during the earliest years of life show up on achievement testing at kindergarten entry. All studies of children's skills have found marked disparities in the cognitive abilities and academic knowledge of children based on their socioeconomic status (see Definition of Socioeconomic Status [SES]) (Lee & Burkam, 2002; Phillips, Brooks-Gunn, Duncan, Klebanov, & Crane, 1998). The average cognitive scores of preschool-aged children in the lowest socioeconomic group are 60% lower than the average scores of children in the highest socioeconomic group (Lee & Burkam, 2002). These *achievement gaps* in

---

Definition of Socioeconomic Status (SES)

A measure of an individual's or family's economic and social position relative to others, based on *income, education,* and *occupation.* When analyzing a family's SES, the household wage earner's education and occupation are examined, as well as combined income. SES is typically broken into three categories: high SES, middle SES, and low SES. These categories describe the three areas a family or an individual may fall into. When placing a family or individual into one of these categories, any or all of the three variables (income, education, and occupation) can be assessed.

---

academic achievement and school performance are significant at school entry—sometimes more than a year's difference—and are persistent throughout kindergarten through Grade 12 (K-12) schooling and even into the postsecondary years. One of the primary goals of the No Child Left Behind Act, signed into law in 2002, is to reduce this achievement gap so that all children will succeed academically and become skilled, productive citizens.

The research on how to reduce this achievement gap has consistently identified early education as one of the most cost-effective methods for improving the school and life outcomes for children from low-income backgrounds. There is a large body of compelling and convincing research indicating that high-quality early interventions can significantly help to reverse these patterns of low achievement and reduced educational attainment (Barnett, 2002; Brooks-Gunn, Rouse, & McLanahan, 2007; Reynolds et al., 2001). Several well-designed, longitudinal, scientifically rigorous studies have all confirmed the cost-effectiveness of reaching out to families during the preschool years and providing systematic, intentional curricula that engage children with challenging content, social support, and frequent rich language interactions (Reynolds et al., 2001; Schweinhart et al., 2005; Gormley et al., 2005).

Parent and family support has also been identified as important to program effectiveness. In addition, these same studies have emphasized the importance of employing highly qualified teachers who are able to individualize and adapt specific instructional strategies based on the strengths and needs of each child in classrooms that are not overly structured or regimented (Espinosa, 2003; Klein & Knitzer, 2006; Pianta, Cox, & Snow, 2007).

INCREASING LINGUISTIC DIVERSITY IN EARLY CHILDHOOD PROGRAMS

Children whose home language is not English or who primarily speak a language other than English in the home are considered *English language learners* (ELLs), dual language learners (DLLs), or *linguistic-minority* (LM) *students.* DLL or ELL children vary greatly as a group in terms of country of origin, recency of immigration, family SES, and specific home language. All of these factors influence the child's adjustment to an educational setting, the rate of English acquisition, and long-term academic achievement (Espinosa, 2007b).

Nationwide, ELL children enrolled in Head Start speak the following languages at home in order of frequency: Spanish (84%), followed by East Asian languages, Middle Eastern/South Asian languages, European/Slavic languages, Native Central/South American and Native Mexican languages, Pacific Island languages, African languages, Caribbean languages, and Native North American/Alaska Native languages (Office of Head Start, 2008). Increasingly, Head Start programs across the nation are serving children from multiple language backgrounds, with 36 states serving more than 8 language groups. Almost all Head Start grantees (85%) serve children and families whose primary language is not English, while a significant number of programs serve families with 8 or more different languages (Office of Head Start, 2008). The diversity of languages represented in our programs means that all early childhood educators will need strategies that have been proven effective for children in the early stages of learning English. Unfortunately, most early educators speak only one language and do not feel adequately prepared to address the needs of ELL children (Ray, Bowman, & Robbins, 2006).

Recent immigrant households and undocumented individuals[1] are the most likely to have limited English fluency, low levels of formal education, and low family incomes (Crosnoe & Lopez-Gonzalez, 2005). Most recent immigrants who are not fluent in English are from Mexico and speak Spanish, although the proportion of all immigrants from Asia has increased to 25% (Dinan, 2006). Currently the *gateway states* (California, Florida, Illinois, New Jersey, New York, and Texas) still account for the majority of the immigrant population (70%); some southern and midwestern states are also witnessing a rapid growth in their immigrant ELL population (Capps, Fix, & Reardon-Anderson, 2003; Office of Head Start, 2008; Hernandez, 2004). Further, many small communities, particularly in the Midwest, have experienced significant influxes of immigrant families in the last decade. For example, in several rural communities in Missouri the percentage of children who do not speak English in the home has risen by more than 500%. Many educators and social service providers have reported feeling overwhelmed and unable to respond effectively to the language needs of these new immigrant populations (Cambio de Colores, 2007).

In a nationally representative study of more than 22,000 children who entered kindergarten in 1998, 68% of the children were classified as English speaking and 18.1% were classified as LM children (Early Childhood Longitudinal Study of Kindergarten Children, ECLS-K) (Espinosa, Laffey, & Whittaker, 2006a). Almost 13% of the total was classified as Spanish speaking, with 2.7% identified as Asian speaking and 2% as speaking a European language. The majority of the LM children were in the two lowest groups for household SES (52%); a most remarkable finding was that 80% of the Spanish speakers judged to be the least fluent in English were also in the lowest SES groups (Espinosa et al., 2006a). This means that Spanish-speaking children who are learning English as a second language during the preschool years are the most likely of all preschool children to live in poverty and have a mother or guardian without a high school education. These data are similar to other studies showing that non-English-proficient children are about twice as likely to live in poverty as English-proficient children in kindergarten through Grade 5 (K-5) and only about 50% have parents with a high school education (Capps et al., 2003).

Increases in Hispanic/Latino Population

The Latino/Hispanic[2] population is the largest and fastest growing ethnic minority group in the United States (U.S. Census Bureau, 2004). There are now more Latinos (almost 40 million) than African Americans (almost 39 million) or any other ethnic group; they represent about 14% of the total population in the nation. By 2050 it

---

[1]Undocumented individuals are those who have entered the United States without the proper documents required to live in or work in this country.

[2]The terms *Hispanic* and *Latino* are used interchangeably throughout this book and refer to people whose origins are from Spain, the Spanish-speaking countries of Central or South America, or the Caribbean. Origin can be viewed as ancestry, nationality, or country of birth of the person or person's parents or ancestors prior to their arrival in the United States. Hispanic/Latino people may be of any race.

has been estimated that the number of Latino children under 5 will increase by 146% and the number of Hispanic and Black children under age 5 will outnumber non-Hispanic White children. This will result in a country where children who have traditionally been classified as racial/ethnic minorities will become the majority group.

Rising immigration rates combined with higher birth rates for Latina women have contributed to increasing numbers of young ELL children entering early care settings. In the United States, the number of young children whose home language is not English has been steadily increasing since the 1980s. It is estimated that approximately 20% of the school-age population speaks a language other than English at home. Between 14% and 16% of all children speak Spanish as their home language (Reyes & Moll, 2006) and another 4% to 6% speak a language other than Spanish. Looking just within the younger K-5 population of ELLs, the majority (76%) speak Spanish and are considered Latino/Hispanic (Capps, Fixx, Ost, Reardon-Anderson, & Passel, 2004). Within the preschool population, this percentage is even higher because of the high fertility and immigration rates of Spanish-speaking families (Lopez, Barrueco, & Miles, 2006).

The percentage of Latino children, as a proportion of all young children, has also been steadily increasing. Currently, Hispanics make up about 22% of all children under the age of 5 (Calderon, Gonzalez, & Lazarin, 2004). Approximately 25% of all live births in 2003 were Hispanic/Latino (Lopez, Barrueco, & Miles, 2006). Of these infants, the majority (~75%) are exposed to Spanish in the home. The children of immigrants will account for 88% of the growth in the under-18 population between 2000 and 2050; the number of Latino children under 5 will increase by 146% (U.S. Department of Health and Human Services, 2001).

In the early childhood community there is a growing research base about the prevalence, parenting practices, early learning conditions, and educational needs

Children from all backgrounds have opportunities to play together and learn from one another in early education programs.

of young Hispanics who grow up learning two languages (see the National Task Force on Early Childhood Education for Hispanics reports; Espinosa, 2007a, 2007b, 2008a). However, there is relatively little published research on young ELLs who grow up in homes that do not speak either English or Spanish.

These dramatic increases in linguistic diversity during the early childhood years have implications for the composition, professional preparation, and training of the workforce. In addition, these highlight the need for improved instructional and assessment approaches that are better suited to this growing population. Clearly, we will need more early childhood teachers and staff who are fluent in multiple languages, but that staffing need may take decades to achieve. In the meantime, all early educators will need to be retrained to better understand the process of first and second language development, how this interacts with poverty and early language-learning environments, and how to improve the school achievement of ELL children. In addition to increased linguistic diversity, early childhood programs are witnessing growing cultural diversity (Lynch & Hanson, 2004).

CULTURE AND EARLY EDUCATION

Culture, with all its processes and functions, is a subject on which we need all the enlightenment we can achieve. . . .

RUTH BENEDICT, 1934

Culture has been described as a shared, learned, symbolic system of values, beliefs, and attitudes that shapes and influences perception and behavior. In essence, it is a lens through which each of us views and interprets the world (Lynch & Hanson, 2004). Research has repeatedly shown that cultural groups vary in their early socialization patterns, their earliest language and literacy practices, as well as their beliefs and approaches to parenting (Lynch & Hanson, 2004; McNaughton, 2005). The types of activities and the frequency of such activities such as book reading or storytelling vary both across cultural groups and within cultural groups. All families differ in some respects from one another. Families use oral and written language in specific ways that help to define and express cultural and social identity (Gee, 2001).

Psychological anthropology defines *culture* as having two dimensions: overt and covert (Hall, 1977). The *overt culture* includes values and norms embedded in language, religion, philosophy, custom, and family practices (Huang, 1997). For instance, within some Asian and Pacific Islander groups, families see teachers as professionals with authority over their children's education; they do not believe that parents should interfere with the schooling process. Consequently, these parents may not understand that they are expected to volunteer in classrooms and participate in events like parent–teacher conferences. *Covert* or *hidden culture,* on the other hand, is defined by the unconscious behavioral and perceptual patterns resulting from daily social learning. For example, many Latino families indirectly teach their children that it is disrespectful to make direct eye contact with authority figures such as teachers. These children may have difficulty looking directly at teachers during conversations; teachers can mistakenly interpret this lack of eye

---

Two Important Aspects of Culture for Early Childhood Educators

1. Specific early child-rearing, language, and literacy practices that are typical of certain cultural groups carry meaning and are important for that group. For example, some Latino groups frequently tell stories, folk tales, and personal anecdotes to teach life lessons like the importance of cooperation and the family. Adults will often sing a song or convey a *dicho* (saying) to make a point with a child.
2. Cultural practices vary greatly across groups and within subgroups. Not all Latino families employ the use of storytelling and *dichos* to convey important life lessons to their children.

---

contact as avoidance or lack of interest. Both aspects of a group's cultural identity will shape a family's behavior in important ways that influence their children's development and acquisition of school-related skills. Some child-rearing practices have their roots in culture and shape how young children interpret the world (see the box above).

Thus, it is important to understand both what constitutes typical patterns of socialization practices for cultural groups (for example, the typical education values associated with Mexican immigrant families) and what constitutes highly individual family patterns of behavior (for instance, how often a particular family reads storybooks to its young children or tells personal stories). Latino and Asian ethnic groups are the largest growing segments of culturally diverse ELLs. They are relatively new populations of children and families who constitute the largest proportion of the new demographics. The following is some general information about Latino, Asian, and African American cultural practices that are relevant to early education:

LATINOS Latinos are much more likely to speak their native language—Spanish—at home than are other ethnic groups (Rumberger & Larson, 1998). They are less likely to have a fluent English-speaking adult in the household; consequently, Latino children enter school with less English fluency and have more difficulty acquiring English proficiency than their peers (National Center for Education Statistics, 2003). Most Hispanic parents report a strong desire for their children to maintain their native language while also learning English (Children Now, 2005). This finding, however, is also influenced by country of origin and social class of the family. The use of Spanish has traditionally served as a culturally unifying aspect of Latino family life as well as a potential social and economic resource. It will nevertheless be important to take the time to discover the preferences and values of individual families without making any assumptions based on ethnicity.

> *Early childhood teachers* will need to interview each family to determine which language is spoken most often in the home and each family's feelings about maintaining its home language and acquiring English. (See Appendix A, Sample Family Languages and Interests Survey).

Latino families have been characterized as sharing a set of values that include the following: *familia*/familism or family-centeredness, *respeto* or respect, *cariño* or nurturance, *responsibilidad* or personal sense of responsibility, and *educación* or formal education (Delgado-Gaitan, 2004; Valdés, 1996). The Hispanic emphasis on family loyalty, solidarity, and mutual obligations has been recognized for decades (Espinosa, 1995; Rothenberg, 1995). The focus on the *familia* is one of the most striking values of the Latino culture. It promotes strong connections to both the immediate and the extended family. This value has been found consistently across the majority of Latino families regardless of country of origin, acculturation, and SES (Bulcroft, Carmody, & Bulcraft, 1996; Fuligni, Tseng, & Lam, 1999; Portes & Zady, 2002). Included in this belief is the expectation that the family will be the major source of both practical and emotional support as well the collective base of loyalty and solidarity.

The term *familia* usually goes beyond the nuclear family. The Latino "family unit" most often includes not only parents and children but also the extended family. In most Hispanic families, the father is the head of the family and the mother is responsible for the home. Individuals within a family have a moral responsibility to aid other members of the family experiencing financial problems, unemployment, poor health conditions, and other life issues. When early childhood teachers are recruiting family support, it is important to include all family members, such as grandparents, aunts, uncles, and so on, as part of the child's support system.

Latino family ties are typically very strong. When someone travels to another town or city to study or for a short visit (e.g., vacation, business, medical reasons), staying with relatives or even with friends of relatives is a common practice. Families often gather together to celebrate holidays, birthdays, baptisms, first communions, graduations, and weddings. Hispanic families instill in their children the importance of honor, good manners, and respect for authority and the elderly.

Several studies have found that Latino families report higher levels of cohesiveness and less parent–child conflict than other ethnic or European American families (Knight, Virdin, & Roosa, 1994). This emphasis on the *familia* also leads to parents exerting more extrafamilial control (e.g., stricter curfews) and encouraging children to spend most of their time at home or with family members. It appears that as children become more assimilated and fluent in English, their commitment to this value weakens. Portes and Rumbaut (2001) found that Latino children of immigrants who were predominantly English

> **Recommendation**
>
> While interviewing Hispanic families, early childhood teachers can discuss the consequences of shifting to an English-only household versus maintaining a bilingual language environment.

speakers were less *familistic* than their bilingual or native-speaking peers. Maintaining the home language for Hispanic families appears to be associated with continuing to promote traditional values. While *adding* English to the home language does not appear to weaken family values, *replacing* home language with English is associated with a decreased commitment to *familia.*

Traditional Latino culture also emphasizes the value of respect (*respeto*). Respect includes both respect for the self (i.e., self-dignity) and others (honoring the dignity of others). Researchers have described the high value that Latino families put on politely greeting elders, not challenging an elder's point of view, entering adult conversations only when invited, not interrupting others, and recognizing the needs of others (Valdés, 1996). Hispanic children are raised to respect other family members as well as the family roles such as father and mother. Children are expected to act respectfully toward siblings, parents, and extended family members because of the position they hold in the family. For example, it would be considered disrespectful for a teenage girl to show signs of affection with her boyfriend in front of a brother or father because it would be considered an offense to the role of brother or father (Manning, 2005).

Within the Latino parenting literature, the goal of *educación*, or *bien educado*, is stressed. The meaning of these terms encompasses more than just formal schooling, degrees, or book learning. When Latinos describe someone as *bien educado,* they mean someone who displays *respeto*, has good manners, high morals, and behaves in accordance with his or her role (sister, mother, father, brother, and so on). Children who are *bien educado* are seen as honest, polite, responsible, and deferential to authority (Delgado-Gaitan, 2004). Latina mothers have been found to view teaching their children morals and appropriate behavior as their primary responsibility, which they began early through the telling of moral tales or *consejos.* Researchers have also found that Latino parents highly value *educación* (Okagaki & Frensch, 1998) and want to be involved in their children's schooling (Lopez, 2001). However, Hispanic parents often face barriers to meaningful school involvement and their culturally preferred ways of supporting their children's achievement may not be consistent with traditional school expectations.

ASIAN AMERICAN   The term *Asian American* covers a variety of national, cultural, and religious heritages. Indeed, Asian Americans represent more than 29 distinct subgroups that differ in language, religion, and customs. The four major groups of Asian Americans are as follows:

- East Asian, such as Chinese, Japanese, and Korean;
- Pacific Islander including Filipinos;
- Southeast Asian, such as Thai and Vietnamese; and
- South Asian, such as Indian and Pakistani (Pang, 1990).

East Asian languages make up an increasing percentage of the non-English languages spoken in early education programs, including Head Start classrooms.

Although there are similarities among the various Asian subgroups, they also vary greatly internally. In addition to between-group differences, as with all cultural groups, diversity exists among individuals. Differences have been found in reasons for migration, related hopes and expectations, and reception by the dominant culture. Some immigrants are refugees from countries torn apart by war, others from the middle class of stable countries. Some came with limited resources and low levels of education, others with skills and affluence (Brand, 1987).

Asian American children are a diverse group. Contrary to popular misconceptions, not all are superior students; some have various kinds of learning difficulties. Some lack motivation, proficiency in English, or financial resources; others have parents who do not understand the American school system because of cultural differences, language barriers, or their more immediate quest for survival (Yao, 1988). In fact, the Asian American population has been described as having "profound inter- and interethnic differences" (Chan & Lee, 2004, p. 221). Some Asian children, struggling with a new language and culture, find American schools very difficult and eventually drop out. Although diversity among groups makes overall descriptions difficult, there are general cultural characteristics, values, and practices shared by most Asians, particularly East and Southeast Asians, that are different from the mainstream American culture.

In many East and Southeast Asian cultures, Confucian ideals, which include respect for elders, deferred gratification, and discipline, are a strong influence. Most Asian American parents teach their children to value educational achievement, respect authority, feel responsibility for relatives, and show self-control (Chan & Lee, 2004). Asian American parents tend to view school failure as a lack of will and address this problem by increasing parental restrictions. Asian American children tend to be more dependent, conforming, and willing to place family welfare over individual wishes than are other American children. These traits reflect traditional Asian values that stress mutual interdependence, conformity, cooperation, and nonconfrontation with indirect communication styles (Lynch & Hanson, 2004).

Self-effacement, the avoidance of drawing attention to oneself combined with personal modesty, is a trait traditionally valued in many Asian cultures. In addition, children who fail to fulfill their primary responsibilities are often reminded that misbehavior reflects poorly on the whole family and the family name; this may lead to "loss of face" (Chan & Lee, 2004). In classrooms, Asian children raised in traditional households tend to wait to participate, unless otherwise requested by the teacher. Having attention drawn to oneself, for example, having one's name put on the board for misbehaving, can bring considerable distress. Many Asian children have been socialized to listen more than speak, to speak in a soft voice, and to be modest in dress and behavior.

Teachers in Asian culture are accorded a higher status than teachers in the United States. Asian American children may thus be confused by the informality between American teachers and students; they expect considerable structure and organization. Further, Asian children tend to need reinforcement from teachers and work more efficiently in a well-structured, quiet environment (Baruth & Manning, 1992).

Clearly, traditional Asian values, child-rearing practices, and attitudes toward education vary widely and are transformed as families are exposed to American culture. Again, to effectively teach children from Asian backgrounds, it is essential for early educators to deepen their knowledge about the complex and dynamic Asian culture in general, as well as the specific cultural practices, customs, values, and aspirations that define the individual families served. When Asian children are from low-income families or do not speak English, many of the recommendations and strategies suggested in this book may be highly appropriate. However, care must be taken to adapt these procedures when necessary based on knowledge of specific family preferences or cultural traditions.

AFRICAN AMERICAN Although the focus of this book is children from poverty backgrounds and children who speak a language other than English in the home, most of whom are Latino or Asian, African American or Black children also represent distinct cultural backgrounds. The people we refer to in the United States as African Americans have their roots in Africa. The U.S. government officially has classified African Americans as having origins in any of the Black racial groups of Africa. Most immigrated from Central and West African tribes, including Ashantis,

Bantu, Efiks, Hausas, Ibos, Krus, Mandingo, Sengalese, and Yorubas (Bennett, 1966; Willis, 2004). By far, the majority of African Americans in the United States have ancestors who immigrated to America against their will as slaves. It has been estimated that 4 million Africans were forcibly removed from their homeland and brought to North America between the 15th and 19th centuries (Willis, 2004). Although most contemporary African Americans descended from this ancestry, it is important to remember that as in all cultural/ethnic groups there are enormous differences among individuals. In fact, some African Americans came as indentured servants in the 17th century and some free African Americans men and women immigrated to America from the West Indies and Africa (Stewart, 1996).

More recently, Africans are immigrating to America again. From Senegal, Ghana, Ethiopia, Mali, Nigeria, Eritrea, and Somalia, Africans are leaving their homelands and making new lives in the United States. These new arrivals are coming in great numbers; more than 500,000 Africans came in the 1990s alone, more than had come in all the 150 years before. These more recent African immigrants are coming for a variety of reasons; some are escaping war-torn countries to create a better, secure life for their children, but many are affluent and are among the most educated immigrants in the United States today.

In 2002 nearly one half (48%) of all African American families were married-couple families compared to 82% of non-Hispanic White families (McLoyd, Hill, & Dodge, 2005). During this period, almost half (48%) of all African American children were living with a single mother; this compares to 16% of non-Hispanic White children living with a single mother (Fields, 2003). African American families also tend to be larger than White families, with 20% of African American families having five or more members while 12% of White families have five or more members (McLoyd et al., 2005). African American families are also much more likely to live in high poverty (i.e., those in which at least 40% of the residents were poor), inner city communities than White families.

Question: What do you think are the consequences of growing up in neighborhoods where many of the families are low income? How might the experiences of children from poor neighborhoods differ from children growing up in more affluent communities?

When considering the complexity of cultural influences, it is important to include the social context in which young African American children are growing up. Race is a powerful aspect of one's personal identity, particularly for African Americans. As Boyd-Franklin (2003, p. 261) has stated, "many African American families' perceptions of the world—including self-identity, racial pride, child rearing, educational and school-related experiences, job or employment opportunities, or lack of them, financial security or the lack of it, as well as treatment in interpersonal encounters and male-female relationships—are screened through the lens of the racial experience."

Knowing about the specific cultural background of children from different ancestries can be helpful to a more accurate understanding of children's behavior. It is important, however, to avoid stereotyping individuals based on their race, culture, or ethnicity. The following information about African American culture should be considered a guideline rather than a template for understanding children and families, because generalizing about groups can reinforce negative stereotypes and prejudices. As each family is unique, it is important when working with children and families from different cultural groups that we learn about and acknowledge the influence of their particular cultural and group history while also learning about the specific details of individual family patterns.

Although the diversity within African American families makes it impossible to generalize about value systems, lifestyles, and social class structure, there are some common themes that run throughout. African Americans are often raised in extended families that provide many opportunities for social interaction (Hale, 1983; McLoyd et al., 2005). Children raised in highly social contexts are often sensitive to nonverbal communications, good at interpreting facial expressions, and emotionally expressive (Shade & Edwards, 1987). One prominent researcher (Hale, 1983, 2001) believes that this people-oriented style of African American child rearing reflects the African heritage. Children within these extended families often have "multiple mothering" in which parenting responsibilities are shared by grandparents, aunts, uncles, cousins, older siblings, or even nonblood relatives such as friends, neighbors, or ministers (Logan, 2001).

Cultural Misunderstanding

Early in my career as a school administrator, I was hired as the principal for a model early childhood program that served children from preschool through Grade 2. The school had been reconfigured under the court-ordered desegregation plan in a large metropolitan district. The community we served was almost exclusively African American and situated in the midst of a low-income, high-crime, inner city neighborhood.

Frequently when we contacted parents about conduct problems with the young children, mothers and/or fathers would arrive at the school with paddles or belts and advise us to spank, paddle, or thrash the misbehaving child. As a young, highly educated early childhood professional, I was well versed in the research about the negative consequences of corporal punishment on children's development. Therefore, I became quite concerned when I witnessed parents speaking harshly to their young children or describing their belief in striking an unruly preschooler as an effective discipline method.

During this time, as part of my own education, I attended a large cultural gathering where we discussed effective educational approaches in our inner city communities. I was describing this parenting practice that I found incompatible with what I knew to be "good for children's development." Suddenly, a local African American minister interrupted me and declared, "How dare you judge how we discipline our children? You have no right to criticize what you don't understand. We have used these methods for centuries because they are necessary. When we were slaves, we had to physically punish our youngsters to prevent them from being treated even more savagely by the White plantation owners. This has been a matter of life and death for us. You cannot interfere with our family values that have served us for centuries."

As a result of this exchange, I was forced to rethink both my approach to discipline within the school and my parenting classes offered to the community.

Question

How do you think you would respond to this dilemma and what are the important considerations when resolving cultural conflicts?

Historically, many African American families have depended on and gained strength from their spiritual and/or religious orientation (Walsh, 2003). Older generations have joined community churches at high rates and often express a sense of connectedness with a "church family" (Boyd-Franklin, 2003). The church community often provides a network of friends and male and female role models who have achieved social stature such as the minister and church elders. For many African American families, the church has provided a source of support and assistance in child rearing.

Many African American families have also reported the use of corporal punishment when disciplining their children (Boyd-Franklin et al., 2000). They have adopted practices that reflect the belief that if you "spare the rod," you "spoil the child." This parenting practice may seem harsh to most early childhood professionals, but "this parenting practice is often rooted in feelings of love and concern in families who fear for their children's well-being, particularly that of their male children" (Boyd-Franklin, 2003, p. 270). The tendency to misunderstand the meaning of more physical methods of discipline in African American families is illustrated in the preceding personal anecdote.

Question: How can knowledge about the cultural background of one group lead to negative stereotyping and how might you avoid this practice?

PRESCHOOL ENROLLMENT AND ELLs

Preschool-aged Latino children are the least likely of any ethnic/racial group to enroll in preschool or child care in the nation. For example, across all racial groups, close to half of the California's children aged 3 to 5 are enrolled in preschool/childcare (47%) while only 37% of Latinos aged 3 to 5 are similarly enrolled (Lopez & de Cos, 2004). When Latino preschoolers live in a household where no one over the age of 14 speaks English fluently (linguistically isolated), the enrollment rate further drops to 32%. In contrast, about 50% of Asian children in California attend preschool or child care irrespective of the ability of persons over the age of 14 to speak English fluently. The language of the home appears to differentially affect participation in group care and education during the preschool years (Espinosa, 2007b).

The reasons behind differential participation rates need to be more clearly understood before effective responses can be designed. However, there are some data suggesting that Latino children attend preschool and/or child care at lower rates because of lack of access and financial constraints, not because of any cultural reluctance among Hispanics and Latinos to enroll their children in group care settings (Fuller, 2005; Hernandez, 2006). In fact, some early care programs in California that serve primarily Hispanic ELLs are consistently overenrolled and have long waiting lists (Espinosa & Lessar, 1993). A recent study in Chicago further supports this conclusion: "Latina mothers needing child care generally viewed child care centers favorably; the fact that few Latinos used child

> Latino children attend preschool and/or child care at lower rates because of lack of access and financial constraints, not because of any cultural reluctance among Hispanics and Latinos to enroll their children in early childhood settings (Fuller, 2005; Hernandez, 2006).

care centers is because affordable center care is not available in their neighbor-hoods" (Illinois Facilities Fund, 2003, p. 4). A comprehensive analysis of immigrant families' enrollment in early education programs has concluded that the primary causes for underenrollment are related to socioeconomic barriers, not cultural bar-riers (Hernandez, 2006). Hernandez also points out that more than 80% of Native Mexican children in Mexico attend some kind of a preschool program while only 55% of immigrant Mexicans attend preschool in the United States. It appears that the cost, the location, ineffective outreach, and lower levels of English language fluency all appear to be major reasons why ELL families are not enrolling their children in early education programs at the same rates as families with different ethnic, cultural, and language backgrounds.

EARLY EDUCATION STANDARDS MOVEMENT AND DIVERSITY

Across the country, state departments of education are designing early learning standards that identify the expectations for what a young child should know and be able to do prior to kindergarten entry. Many of these learning expectations are based on current research focused on the early skills learned in preschool that pre-dict later literacy, mathematical knowledge, and academic achievement. With the current emphasis on educational accountability, outcomes for children, and re-search-based classroom practices, these standards help to provide a focus to the curriculum and guidance to teachers about what to teach and when to teach it (Kagan, Kauerz, & Tarrant, 2007). They also identify the important teaching and learning objectives that need to be included in an assessment system.

For example, most states have identified a set of language standards that in-clude vocabulary, syntax (grammar), speaking, and specific early reading skills that relate to later reading fluency such as alphabet knowledge, phonological awareness, and print awareness. All of these skills, which are typically learned during the preschool years, have been found to be important for later reading abil-ity and achievement, the cornerstone of academic achievement (Dickinson & Tabors, 2001; National Early Literacy Panel, 2008). Examples of language standards include the following:

- The child follows two- and three-step directions (Florida).
- The child listens and speaks effectively in a variety of situations (Illinois).
- The child will develop an understanding of words and word meanings through the use of appropriate vocabulary (Virginia).
- The child uses age-appropriate grammar in conversations and increasingly complex phrases and sentences (Florida).
- The child develops age-appropriate phonological awareness (California).

These standards or expectations are based on the extensive research that has been conducted on English-speaking monolingual children. This research ad-dresses both what typically developing children *can* learn during the preschool years and specifically which of these skills are most important to later, more com-plex literacy abilities (National Early Literacy Panel, 2008).

Although the development of learning standards for very young children has many critics (Meisels, 2007; Parini, 2005) and carries with it the dangers of

Many states expect early childhood teachers to teach young children specific early language and literacy skills that will prepare them for kindergarten.

inappropriate testing and narrowing of the curriculum to reflect only measurable outcomes (Pianta et al., 2007), it is an undeniable aspect of the early childhood movement in this country. Whether we like it or not, educational policy makers, legislators, and the public want to know if our early interventions are teaching our youngest students what they need to know to successfully master the rigors of formal education. It is now a question of *getting it right.* To best serve the needs of the children and families who enter our programs with so much hope and potential, we must design curriculum, assessment, and accountability systems that accurately and fairly represent the capabilities and educational needs of *all* our children (Espinosa & Lopez, 2007).

A pressing question for early childhood policy makers, program administrators, and teachers is how to apply these standards to children who are learning English as a second language and are being raised in homes where the cultural norms and practices are quite diverse. To what extent do the learning expectations for monolingual, U.S.-born, English-speaking children reflect the developmental progression of ELL children? Unfortunately, the comparable research for young ELL children is meager at best (August & Shanahan, 2006). We have a sizeable amount of information about the process and stages of first- and second language acquisition that extends back to the early 20th century (Genessee, Paradis, & Crago, 2004). However, we have only a handful of rigorous studies that have empirically documented

> It is now a question of *getting it right.* . . . we must design curriculum, assessment, and accountability systems that accurately and fairly represent the capabilities and educational needs of *all* our children (Espinosa & Lopez, 2007).

the impact of preschool on ELL children, the relative effectiveness of different curricular approaches, the rates of English acquisition for children from low-income non-English-speaking homes, or how to best capitalize on the native language strengths of young ELL children (August & Shanahan, 2006; Para Nuestros Niños, 2006).

Fortunately, much of the emerging information is consistent and overwhelmingly leads to similar conclusions. Although the amount of research information is not as extensive as we would like, the findings from small, descriptive studies as well as larger national studies are remarkably similar. The same themes run throughout the preschool, kindergarten through Grade 3 (K-3), and K-12 literature on how to best educate ELL students to high achievement levels in English:

1. High-quality instruction with adaptations seems to have the most impact on ELL children. These adaptations include special attention to English vocabulary and English oral language development, lots of opportunities for practice, and organized peer interactions with English-speaking children (August & Shanahan, 2006; Espinosa, Castro, Crawford, & Gillanders, 2007; Para Nuestros Niños, 2006).
2. Schools need to build systematic connections to families in order to design curricular approaches that are culturally consistent and to build on the strengths of ELL children and families.
3. Support for the home language is critical. These include language interactions, literacy activities, and to the maximum extent possible, some instruction in the child's dominant language.
4. Qualified teachers and support staff who are fluent in the child's home language as well as knowledgeable about the cultural practices of the families should be recruited and hired.
5. Special attention needs to be given to the maintenance of the child's home language, which often means working with families so that children do not lose their home languages.

Subsequent chapters will address these findings in more depth and with detailed suggestions for translating these research findings into practical classroom strategies. The scientific evidence reviewed here and in future chapters provides a compelling rationale for *why* we need to intervene early in the lives of young ELLs and children from low-income households. Chapters 4, 5, and 6 describe in more detail *how* we can best use this knowledge to design effective programs, classrooms, and curriculum.

Summary

We know that the numbers and proportion of young children from diverse socioeconomic, linguistic, and cultural backgrounds is rapidly increasing. We also know that children from these backgrounds have historically been at risk for academic delays and reduced educational outcomes. The federal government, in cooperation with state education agencies, has recently instituted rigorous achievement standards that all schools must meet for all children, including preschool and primary-aged children. Finally, the weight of research demonstrates that high-quality early education is a cost-effective intervention when well designed, well resourced, and initiated early enough to take advantage of the amazing plasticity of the growing brain.

At this juncture in educational policy making and program implementation, we need to clearly articulate the specific teaching strategies, curriculum models, and assessment approaches that have been shown to be effective with diverse groups of children. We need to apply what we know so that children from impoverished homes, children who are learning English as a second language, and children who are growing up in culturally diverse families will thrive and benefit from the expanded early educational programs becoming available throughout this country. How can we *get it right* and ensure that all our children benefit from these expanded educational opportunities?

Reflection and Discussion Questions

1. What changes or trends have you observed in your community that might confirm the growing diversity of young children who attend early childhood programs? How have individuals in your community typically responded to these changes?

2. What are the percentages of children who live in poverty or low-income households in your local programs? (You might need to call your local school district or look up these statistics online.) Are there programs that target low-income or "at-risk" children in your community, for example, Head Start or Title I prekindergarten programs?

What are the components of these programs? How do they handle family outreach, eligibility, curriculum design, and child assessment?

3. How many children in your local community do not speak English at home? Do you know how many of them are attending some type of early education program? (These data may be hard to find—you can start by calling either your local district office or state department of education.)

4. Have you ever had an experience with a person from another culture that was confusing for you? If so, please describe what happened and what you learned.

What Research Tells Us About the Needs and Abilities of All Young Children

The need to address significant inequalities in opportunity, beginning in the earliest years of life, is both a fundamental moral responsibility and a critical investment in our nation's social and economic future.

NATIONAL SCIENTIFIC COUNCIL ON THE DEVELOPING CHILD,
*THE SCIENCE OF EARLY CHILDHOOD DEVELOPMENT: CLOSING THE GAP
BETWEEN WHAT WE KNOW AND WHAT WE DO*, 2007b

A recent explosion of research from the neurosciences and related fields concretely demonstrates the powerful influences of early experiences on the growing architecture of the brain. It is now possible to directly record the effects of deprived versus enriched learning environments on the density and location of developing neural pathways. That is, we now know that early learning environments that are chronically stressful, deprived, or harsh can lead to long-term educational and behavioral problems (National Scientific Council on the Developing Child, 2007c); consistent, responsive, and support-ive relationships with important adults are essential for all children. The earliest interactions between a child and his or her environment can have a profound impact on the course of development. Some scientists have called the early years a *sensitive period* for the healthy development of language, vision, hearing, and social responsiveness (Knudsen, Heckman, Cameron, & Shonkoff, 2006). We are coming very close to understanding the behavioral and neurological components of healthy growth and development as well as the environments necessary for vigorous development to occur (National Scientific Council on the Developing Child, 2008).

THE SCIENCE OF EARLY EDUCATION

Complex skills and abilities such as the ability to read, reason, and make inferences are developed over time through successive interactions that build on previous learning. Science has shown that specific brain circuitry is associated with specific sets of skills and that the earliest experiences lay the foundations (neural pathways) that are necessary for later, more complex skill development. Therefore, when a child does not have the opportunity to learn certain concepts when he or she is *neurologically ready* or during the sensitive period (such as an extended vocabulary while language is first developing), more energy and time will be required to learn these same concepts as the child ages (National Scientific Council on the Developing Child, 2007b). This does not mean that complex skills and concepts cannot be learned at older ages, just that it will be more costly and less efficient to learn some skills later in life (see the following definition).

A well-known example of how early language learning opportunities shaped overall development was the case study of Genie, who was described in a series of publications in the 1970s (Rhymer, 1993). Genie was essentially kept in isolation by a neglectful and abusive parent, with no exposure to language and normal social experiences during her early childhood years. When she was discovered, she had some understanding of language but did not speak. After nearly one year of intensive training and instruction, she had a vocabulary of about 200 words and was speaking in two-word sentences. Six years later, she had made much progress, but she was still much less advanced in her language than other children her age who had normal language experiences during this period.

Because Genie was able to acquire some language following the onset of adolescence, the belief that language learning is impossible after the sensitive period could no longer be completely supported. Rather, language learning *can* occur after the sensitive period, but it may be incomplete. The period between

---

Sensitive Period

When the effect of experience on the brain is particularly strong during a limited period in development, this period is referred to as a *sensitive period*. During this period, certain experiences are important for normal development to occur. For example, the sensitive period for language learning is generally believed to be between birth and 6 years of age. During these years, children are particularly receptive to all forms of linguistic input: phonology, vocabulary, grammar, and pragmatics (the appropriate use of language in social situations). Given the high level of receptivity, this is an ideal time for young children to learn the fundamentals of language.

infancy and middle childhood, therefore, is most likely a sensitive period for language learning. That is, language can be acquired more easily during this time and although it is not impossible to learn language later in life, it is considerably more difficult and may not ever reach typical levels of proficiency.

This scientific research has also underscored the *plasticity* of the young brain. *Plasticity* refers to the capacity of the brain to change with experience. Clearly, the brain has most plasticity during the early years and it decreases with age. Early experiences can literally shape the neural circuitry of the brain. During the early years, the brain is in the initial stages of formation; at this stage, brain development is happening at a rapid pace and is amenable to outside influences. Once specific experiences have shaped patterns of neural circuits, they become more established and are less likely to be altered by later, different experiences (National Scientific Council on the Developing Child, 2007c). This means that young children are in need of age-appropriate learning opportunities to build the lower level brain circuits that are the foundation for later, more sophisticated skill development. "Thus early learning lays the foundation for later learning and is essential (though not sufficient) for the development of optimized brain architecture. Stated simply, stimulating early experience must be followed by more sophisticated and diverse experiences later in life, when high-level circuits are maturing, in order for full potential to be achieved" (National Scientific Council on the Developing Child, 2008, p. 4).

The relationship between age, early experiences, and brain formation is illustrated in Figure 3.1. The neural pathways involved with sensory processes such as vision and hearing are most sensitive to environmental shaping during the first months of life. Meanwhile, the neural circuits important to language

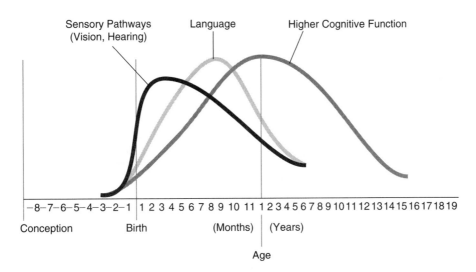

FIGURE 3.1 Human brain development: synapse formation dependent on early experiences.

Source: From *Neurons to Neighborhoods: The Science of Early Childhood Development,* by J. P. Shonkoff & D. A. Phillips (Eds.), 2000, Washington DC: National Academies Press, p. 188. Reprinted with permission from the National Academies Press. Copyright 2000, National Academy of Sciences.

development are being formed during the first year of life; this formation gradually tapers off after about 6 to 7 years of age. A child's experiences during these time periods are critical to the formation of brain circuitry that underlies all development.

BRAIN DEVELOPMENT AND POVERTY   Children who grow up in low-income homes are at greater risk for impaired brain development because they are more likely to be exposed to multiple risk factors. From the earliest stages of development, the growing fetus is susceptible to the adverse effects of inadequate nutrition, substance abuse, maternal depression, exposure to environmental toxins, trauma or abuse, and/or low-quality child care (National Center for Children in Poverty, 1999). The approximately 13 million children who are considered poor are more likely to be exposed to one or more of these environmental conditions that can hinder brain development. Although many children from poor households demonstrate remarkable levels of resilience and are able to overcome environmental hardships, too many are negatively impacted and show delayed development in areas critical for school success. These developmental areas include vocabulary acquisition, language development, early literacy skills, and emotional self-regulation (Brooks-Gunn, Brown, Duncan, & Moore, 1995; Hart & Risley, 1995; Lee & Burkam, 2002).

Prenatal experiences such as inadequate nutrition or exposure to toxins (such as mercury, lead, certain pesticides, alcohol, nicotine, and cocaine) can have profound and long-lasting effects on the developing infant. (See Figure 3.2 for a graphic depiction of the impact of poverty on brain development.) "The

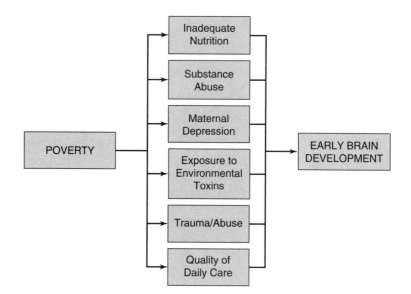

FIGURE 3.2   Impact of poverty on brain development: multiple pathways.

Source: From *Poverty and Brain Development in Early Childhood*, June 1999, New York: National Center for Children in Poverty, Columbia University Mailman School of Public Health. Copyright by the Trustees of Columbia University in the City of New York. Reprinted with permission.

premise underlying this phenomenon, known as *developmental programming*, is that biological events that occur during fetal and postnatal life predispose the child to an elevated risk of subsequent problems in physical and mental health" (National Scientific Council on the Developing Child, 2007c, p. 6). These effects can be as severe as mental retardation or as mild as increased restlessness. Mothers who are living in poverty are also more likely to be depressed. Maternal depression has been linked to less responsive and nurturing care giving, and to babies who are more withdrawn, are less active, and have shorter attention spans (Belle, 1990).

In addition, there has been compelling research documenting the negative impact of poverty on children's language development (Hart & Risley, 1995, 1999). Rapid vocabulary, cognitive, overall language development, and social-emotional growth begins during the second year of life and continues through the preschool years. Children need rich and responsive language interactions, nurturing caregiving, and individualized attention to achieve healthy development during this time. The income and educational levels of families has been shown to directly influence the type, quality, and frequency of early interactions and language experiences (Brookes-Gunn et al., 1995; Hart & Risley, 1995, 1999; Sirin, 2005).

The current knowledge base indicates that children who do not have sufficient language stimulation and interactions during the early years will continue to lag behind their more advantaged peers on measures of language and literacy throughout their school years (see Figure 3.3). This disparity in development, however, can be reduced if high-quality early intervention is provided early, consistently, and with enough intensity (Burchinal et al., 1989; McCartney et al., 2007; Schweinhart

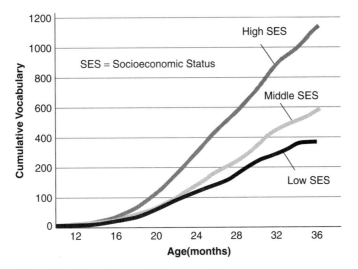

FIGURE 3.3 Disparities in early vocabulary growth.

Source: From *Meaningful Differences in the Everyday Experience of Young American Children,* by B. Hart & T. R. Risley, 1995, Baltimore, MD: Paul H. Brookes, p. 47. Reprinted by permission. http://www.brookespublishing.com/store/books/hart-1979/index.htm.

et al., 2005). Based on the most rigorous and current scientific evidence available, the recently formed National Scientific Center on the Developing Child (2007c) located at Harvard University has concluded the following:

> *The basic concepts of neuroscience and child development research in-dicate that early environments that do not provide such growth-promoting experiences, beginning in early infancy, miss out on key windows of opportunity for building healthy brain architecture and mastering important foundational skills that are building blocks for increasingly complex brain circuits and capacities over time. p. (18)*

Again, early language experiences lay the foundation for later more complex literacy skills. Recent research on early skills that predict future reading fluency and comprehension has shown how important the following skills are to future ac-ademic performance (National Early Literacy Panel Report, 2008):

- the development of an expanded vocabulary,
- the ability to use language flexibly and with fluency,
- the acquisition of knowledge about the world, and
- the ability to use language to think.

For all children, but particularly for children living in poverty, adequate nu-trition, high-quality early care and education, combined with family support, are essential for healthy brain development (Holzer, Schanzenbach, Duncan, & Ludwig, 2007; National Scientific Council on the Developing Child, 2007a).

MULTIPLE LANGUAGES AND BRAIN DEVELOPMENT   Current research on the im-pact of multiple languages on infant brain development is also helping us under-stand how young children in multilingual environments grow and develop (Kuhl, 2004).

We have known for decades that infants learn language rapidly and appar-ently effortlessly. Recent scientific information from neuroscience, biology, and psychology has provided insights about how the infant brain processes perceptual information, learns words and grammar of one or more languages, and the social contexts that promote language acquisition and fluency (Kuhl, 2004; Kuhl, Tsao, & Liu, 2003). This line of research has shown that *all* infants are capable of discern-ing the phonetic (sound) characteristics of all languages from birth, including lan-guages spoken in the home and foreign languages. However, between 6 and 12 months of age, infants' ability to discriminate the sounds (phonetic units) of lan-guages not heard in the infants' environment sharply declines. Evidently, while in-fants are learning the sounds and features of their native language, they are also losing their sensitivity to the sounds of foreign languages. This makes the learning of a foreign language later in life more difficult.

Patricia Kuhl and her colleagues at the Center for Mind, Brain, and Learning at the University of Washington have also found evidence that when infants are exposed to more than one language (which is typical in most parts of the world), the learning occurs in separate neural pathways. As Dr. Kuhl describes it, "Each language is tracking in different parts of the brain" (Kuhl, 2007, CNN News Doc-umentary). These findings suggest "infants have the innate capacity to acquire

Young children learn the features of language through close, personal interactions.

two languages without significant costs to the development of either language. Simultaneous dual language children generally experience the same milestones at approximately the same age as monolingual children, in both the early months and later on with respect to grammatical development" (Genesee, Paradis, & Crago, 2004, p. 84). In addition to the capacity to acquire more than one language, much research has documented the special cognitive, linguistic, and social advantages of bilingualism (Garcia, 2003, 2005; Bialystok, 2001; Genesee et al., 2004). This is one example of how current, credible scientific research can, and should, be applied to guide our educational approach to young children who enter our programs speaking a language other than English. More about this research and its educational implications is discussed in Chapters 5 and 6.

SOCIAL-EMOTIONAL ROOTS OF ALL LEARNING: THE IMPORTANCE OF POSITIVE RELATIONSHIPS

The development of social and emotional competence has been shown to be essential to future academic achievement and social functioning (Bowman, Donovan, & Burns, 2001; Raver, 2002; Shonkoff & Philips, 2000). Research since the 1980s has made it increasingly clear that children's social and emotional adjustment is critically important to their kindergarten readiness and future school success (Smith, 2008). Those who can handle their emotions in acceptable ways and who are able to regulate their behavior are more likely to experience academic success than their peers with emotional and/or behavioral problems. Between birth and 6 years old, young children are acquiring the behavioral, emotional, and cognitive self-control that will allow them to complete complex social and cognitive tasks and interactions (Shonkoff & Philips, 2000). Emotionally well-adjusted children are able to manage powerful emotions constructively and develop the self-regulation to keep attention focused on tasks while inhibiting undesirable behavior. They can handle anger without resorting to aggressive actions; they are able to use their words to resolve conflicts instead of hurtling blocks or books across the room. Quite simply, early emotional development lays the foundation for future mental health and psychological functioning (Shonkoff & Philips, 2000).

The central role of early positive relationships characterized by trust and reciprocity was a major theme of the influential book, *Neurons to Neighborhoods: The Science of Early Childhood Development*, commissioned and published by the National Academies of Science (Shonkoff & Phillips, 2000). In 2003, a team of scientists, including the co-editor of *Neurons to Neighborhoods*, established the Center on the Developing Child at Harvard University and formed the National Scientific Council on the Developing Child (NSCDC). The mission of this council is to "gather, synthesize, and communicate science in support of policies that promote successful learning, adaptive behavior, and sound physical and mental health for all young children" (National Scientific Council on the Developing Child, 2008, p. 1). One of the core concepts of development outlined in an early center paper is that "emotional well-being and social competence provide a strong foundation for emerging cognitive abilities, and together they are the bricks and mortar that comprise the foundation of human development" (National Scientific Council on the Developing Child, 2008, p. 8). This paper also highlighted the critical importance of consistent, supportive relationships for young children who live under conditions of long-term exposure to high levels of stress. Positive relationships help the child to feel safe and cope with adverse conditions.

Social competence includes the ability to form relationships and positive attachments to others (Benard, 2004). Many early childhood experts have long stressed the importance of social abilities that underlie academic learning such as social knowledge of appropriate behavior, emotional self-regulation, and a range of social skills that enable children to interact with one another (Epstein, 2009). Recent research has revealed strong links between social abilities and positive academic outcomes. It has also shown strong associations between antisocial behaviors and poor academic outcomes (Epstein, 2009; Zins, Bloodworth, Weissberg, & Walberg, 2004). The following social skills have been shown to be important to school success (Smith, 2008):

- the ability to get along with and be accepted by others (parents, teachers, and peers);
- the ability to listen to and follow directions;
- the ability to play cooperatively and communicate emotions appropriately; and
- having good feelings about oneself and others.

The development of emotional and social competence occurs in the context of warm, nurturing, and responsive relationships. Literally all development is shaped by the quality of a young child's earliest relationships with primary caregivers (National Scientific Council on the Developing Child, 2007a; Shonkoff & Philips, 2000). All infants are predisposed to develop close emotional bonds with those adults who care for them during their early years. Across all cultures young children form strong attachments and use primary caregivers as sources of security and comfort (Harwood, Miller, & Irizarry, 1995). The social skills described previously are dependent on early, secure attachments with primary caregivers and later through positive, responsive interactions with those in their day-to-day lives. Ron Lally, the co-director of the WestEd Center for Child and Family Studies, has identified "gifts" that high-quality early care programs offer young children: nurturance, support, security, predictability, focus, encouragement, and expansion (Lally, Lurie-Hurvitz, & Cohen, 2006). These gifts foster the child's cognitive development as well as provide a safe and secure place that frees the child's energy for learning.

IMPLICATIONS OF RESEARCH FOR EARLY CHILDHOOD PRACTITIONERS

The most credible and current scientific findings about the environmental conditions that promote healthy development and positive outcomes for children strongly suggest that *all* children ages 3 to 6 need stable, positive, and nurturing relationships from the earliest moments in life. Early childhood teachers can address this need by establishing close, welcoming, and responsive bonds with the children in their classrooms. High-quality programs for young children require early childhood education (ECE) staff who are well trained in both the curriculum to be taught as well as the ability to establish warm and reciprocal relationships with children from all backgrounds. Rich language exposure is critically important during these years and should be a focal point within early childhood classrooms. ECE staff will also need to work closely with parents and other family members to ensure home environments that can sustain the growth-promoting experiences necessary for healthy brain development. The science of early brain development clearly indicates that preschool programs should promote balanced and developmentally appropriate approaches that honor the "whole child" (National Scientific Council on the Developing Child, 2007b). Specific instructional strategies will be discussed in more detail in subsequent chapters; however, the guiding principles for the design of early childhood practices are now clearly illuminated by rigorous scientific evidence.

RESILIENCY AND YOUNG CHILDREN

All young children are endowed with strengths and talents; most face some degree of risk that could threaten their development. In essence, we all have the capacity to thrive and achieve, and we all need some help at different times in our development. The resiliency literature underlines the strengths of all young children. It also emphasizes their potential to overcome childhood adversities with sufficient supports from family, schools, and communities (Benard, 2004; Rutter, 1984, 1993). Through the resiliency lens, unique family and child strengths are emphasized; educators are reminded that we have the ability to foster, nurture, and support each child toward future success. All children have the innate capacity to succeed. Carefully structured learning environments can enhance this capacity.

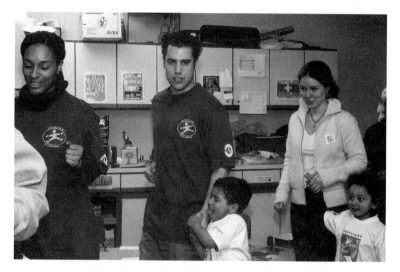

Caring and supportive relationships are important to the development of personal strengths for all children.

The strengths-based approach promoted by the resiliency literature is based on four basic tenets:

1. Resilience is a capacity all children have for healthy development and successful learning.
2. Certain personal strengths are associated with healthy development and successful learning: social competence, problem solving, autonomy, and sense of purpose. These manifestations of resilience and implications for early childhood teachers will be discussed in more detail in Chapter 4.
3. Certain characteristics of families, schools, and communities are associated with the development of personal strengths and, in turn, healthy development and successful learning: caring and supportive relationships, high expectations, and opportunities for participation and meaningful involvement.
4. Changing the life trajectories of children and youth from risk to resilience starts with changing the beliefs of the adults in their families, schools, and communities (Benard, 2004).

I have found the research on the amazing capacity of children to overcome adversity and achieve stable, satisfying lives when sufficient supports are available in the child's environment to be particularly important for teachers who work with children from diverse and/or low-income backgrounds. (See example of a resilient child in box that follows.) In a sense, all development can be characterized as a striving for adaptive coping when confronted with environmental challenges. Children are constantly struggling to learn, energetically processing new information, responding to their emotional needs, and looking to adults to help them understand their world. Fortunately, we now have the scientific evidence that will help design settings that foster resiliency for all children. Chapter 4 summarizes the resiliency literature and describes classroom strategies that early childhood teachers can implement that will promote resilience for all children.

Case Study in Resiliency

While growing up, I had a cousin, Lucy, who lived close to me. She was the fifth of six children in a crowded, chaotic Hispanic family that constantly struggled to pay the rent and purchase the bare necessities of life. The parents were barely 18 when their first child was born and possessed few marketable skills. The household was mostly run by the oldest child, Margarita, who tried to keep up with the cleaning and laundry. She often found very little food to prepare for the other five children. Needless to say, no one in this family ever encouraged the girls to consider a college education or paid much attention to their scholastic talents. Domestic skills were the prized attributes for the girls in this family.

Lucy showed academic ability early in her life. Despite discouragement from her family, she worked hard in school and talked about going to college. Lucy was a petite, dark-haired girl who seemed to charm adults and made friends easily. During her early elementary years, Lucy was often kept home during one domestic crisis or another, so she had frequent school absences. Lucy was fortunate to have teachers who saw her potential and enthusiastically responded to her personality. Somehow during these early years, Lucy came to develop confidence in herself and grew determined that she would "go to school until she had read all the books in the library."

Over time, school was the one place where Lucy felt successful. She was always in the top of her classes and found teachers often expected her to take leadership roles in class activities. Immediately after finishing high school, Lucy left home, applied for a scholarship, and began a college program that took her 6 years to complete as she always had to work at least two jobs to support herself. Although none of her siblings showed any interest in attending college and all her three sisters were married with children by the age of 20, Lucy eventually achieved a graduate degree (with the support of scholarships) and embarked on a highly successful career in education.

Question

In what ways did Lucy demonstrate resilience and how did her environment support or not support her?

Do you know any children like Lucy? If so, what are the conditions of their home and school environments?

USING POTENTIALS TO BUILD CAPACITIES: EDUCATING FOR THE FUTURE

It is clear that too many children have unrealized talents and untapped potentials. Although Warren (from Chapter 1) displayed advanced mathematical abilities, a surprising degree of intellectual focus for a 5-year-old, and the desire to succeed at complex tasks, he also had social and behavioral problems that were interfering with his schooling. Warren needed a caring teacher to recognize his unique blend of talents and needs who could individualize the curriculum and adapt the schedule to allow Warren to achieve success. Most teachers would probably need some help to design an effective program for Warren. But all teachers could start with an appreciation for the remarkable strengths of a troubled child and build a trusting, caring relationship.

The National Commission on Teaching and America's Future (NCTAF) has outlined what it will take to achieve a preschool to college educational system in which every child receives a quality education (National Commission on Teaching and America's Future, 2007). The central question that each program must answer is, What do early childhood teachers in my community need to know and be able to do in order to promote development and learning for all children? The children in our early education programs today are increasingly diverse, exposed to digital media from the earliest ages, and facing a future that is hard to imagine. They often bring with them a background that is unfamiliar and must be educated for a future that will most certainly be dramatically different from the present.

Summary

A rich body of scientific knowledge is available to guide informed early childhood policies and practices. We know that development is a function of both genetic potential and the interactions and experiences early in life that shape the architecture of the brain. "That is to say, the quality of a child's early environment and the availability of appropriate experiences at the right stages of development are crucial in determining the strength or weakness of the brain's architecture, which, in turn, determines how well he or she will be able to think and to regulate emotions" (National Scientific Council on the Developing Child, 2007b, p. 1)

All children need strong and positive bonds with the important adults in their lives; they benefit from sustained and responsive interactions. We now know that the consistent support of a trusted caregiver is critical for children living in adverse circumstances and can bolster resilience in all children. Most children will experience challenging circumstances at some point in their development; school environments can be designed that will enhance their personal resilience. We have the knowledge to improve the life chances of vulnerable young children through effective early educational services that identify and target abilities and strengths as well as needs. The following chapters highlight in more detail specific research findings and offer strategies and recommendations for practitioners.

Reflection and Discussion Questions

1. Why are the early years particularly important for all learning and development?
2. How has the research presented in this chapter influenced your view of your role as an early childhood educator?
3. What types of experiences are essential for young children? Are there any learning and/or teaching opportunities that would best be reserved for older children?
4. What are all the possible ways in which poverty could influence a child's daily life and development?
5. Why do you think the quality of relationships has such profound impacts on children's growth and development?

4

Research Findings and Recommendations for Children Living in Poverty

*If you want to promote good developmental
outcomes for young children . . . don't be poor!*

<small>Anonymous quote at the Language Minority Roundtable
Meeting in Washington, DC, May 2008</small>

To grow and thrive, young children need adequate nutrition, emotionally nurturing relationships and interactions, rich language-learning opportunities, and physical activity. As outlined in Chapter 3, poverty can negatively influence all of these aspects of early development. When young children are growing up in households that struggle daily with having enough money to buy food, medical care, basic housing, and household supplies, they are also more likely to experience neglect, abuse, and excessive stress or trauma. These multiple influences of an impoverished early learning environment can threaten healthy development. However, the current research offers early childhood practitioners the opportunity to positively influence the growth and development of young children who are growing up in disadvantaged circumstances. The impacts of poverty can be significant and enduring, but the power of early childhood programs can also be significant and enduring, if well timed and well designed.

ISSUES AND CONSIDERATIONS
FOR CHILDREN LIVING IN POVERTY

WHO IS POOR?   The federal poverty level in 2008 was $21,200 in annual income for a family of four. (See Chapter 2 for a discussion of how federal poverty rates are calculated.) The National Center for Children Living in Poverty estimates that almost 13 million U.S. families are living below the poverty level and that another 28 million children live in low-income households (National Center for Children Living in Poverty, 2007). A family of four with an annual income below $42,000 is considered low income. This means that low-income families are struggling to meet their basic needs—for example housing, food, transportation, medical services, and clothing. There is very little money left over for additional items like books, toys, videos, music, or trips.

The rates of child poverty vary across the states, with a low of 6% in New Hampshire to a high of 29% in Mississippi (National Center for Children Living in Poverty, 2007). See Figure 4.1 for a view of how poverty varied across the states in 2006. As we are experiencing a new economic downturn, these poverty rates

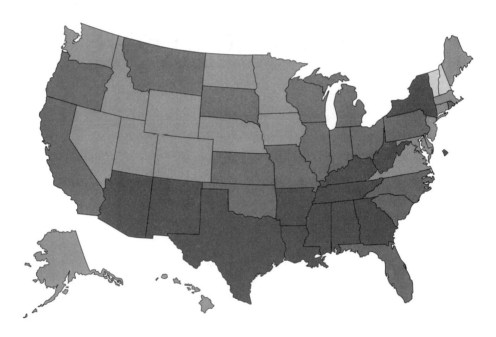

■ 20% or more (13 states): AL, AR, AZ, DC, GA, KY, LA, MS, NM, NY, TN, TX, WV

■ 15-19% (17 states): CA, FL, IL, IN, KS, MI, MO, MT, NC, OH, OK, OR, PA, RI, SC, SD, WI

■ 10-14% (19 states): AK, CO, CT, DE, HI, ID, IA, ME, MD, MA, MN, NE, NV, NJ, ND, UT, VA, WA, WY

□ Under 10% (2 states): NH, VT

FIGURE 4.1   Child poverty rates across the states, 2006.

Source: From *Who Are America's Poor Children?* by S. Fass & N. K. Cauthen, November 2007, New York: National Center for Children in Poverty, Columbia University Mailman School of Public Health. Retrieved September 2008, from www.nccp.org/publications/pub_787.html. Copyright by the Trustees of Columbia University in the City of New York. Reprinted with permission.

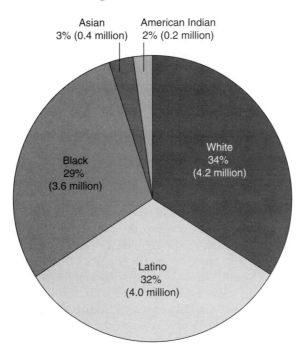

FIGURE 4.2 Poor children by race/ethnicity, 2006.

Source: Who Are America's Poor Children? by S. Fass & N. K. Cauthen, November 2007, New York: National Center for Children in Poverty, Columbia University Mailman School of Public Health. Retrieved September 2008, from www.nccp.org/publications/pub_787.html. Copyright by the Trustees of Columbia University in the City of New York. Reprinted with permission.

will continue to fluctuate; the percentages of children living in poverty will likely increase depending on the depth and duration of the economic recession of 2008 to 2009.

As described earlier in Chapter 2, poverty is more likely in single-parent households or where parents have not graduated from high school. The educational attainment of the head of household is strongly correlated with family income levels. African American, Latino, and American Indian children are also more likely to be living in poor households. Again, the distribution of poverty among different groups varies among racial/ethnic groups (see Figure 4.2). Although proportionately a greater percentage of American Indian (40%), Black (33%), and Latino (27%) children are growing up in poverty, White children still make up the largest number of all children in poverty (National Center for Children Living in Poverty, 2007).

HOW POVERTY INFLUENCES GROWTH AND DEVELOPMENT Decades of research have shown that children who grow up in low-income households are more likely than others to experience academic difficulties throughout their schooling. They are also more likely than others to engage in more problematic behavior and experience employment problems in the future (Zahn-Waxler, Duggal, & Gruber, 2002).

It is not difficult to imagine why children in families who experience persist-ent poverty face many challenges that often compromise their healthy develop-ment. The Center on the Developing Child at Harvard University has documented the negative consequences of inadequate nutrition, deprived early learning oppor-tunities, and unsafe neighborhoods on the developing brain (NSCDC, 2007c). In addition, parents living with economic uncertainty are also vulnerable to depres-sion and other forms of psychological distress, which can adversely affect their ability to be responsive and nurturing with their young children. Sophisticated studies have revealed that children are most susceptible to the impact of poverty during the early childhood years because this is when the brain is most malleable and healthy development in all domains is dependent upon positive, supportive relationships (Duncan & Brooks-Gunn, 1997; Mayer, 1997).

Chronic poverty is associated with more damaging impacts on children's overall development than episodic poverty. Children who are growing up in fam-ilies that are chronically poor show more behavior problems and lower cognitive performance than those who are growing up in homes that are poor during some but not all of the child's early years. By comparing families who were never poor or poor during certain periods of the child's life with those who were chronically poor, the National Institute of Child Health and Human Development Early Child Care Research Network (2005) was able to show the connections between chronic poverty and lower quality child-rearing environments. The authors were able to demonstrate that poverty was associated with less positive parenting practices and less favorable family situations, which in turn were associated with worse out-comes for children. Children who lived in families that were never poor had the best cognitive and behavioral outcomes (National Institute of Child Health and Human Development Early Child Care Research Network, 2005).

Other large-scale studies have also found that certain dimensions of the home child-rearing environment are closely linked to the depressed cognitive and social development of children who live in chronic poverty (Korenman, Miller, & Sjaastad, 1994). Specific aspects of the child-rearing environment such as availabil-ity of stimulating toys, books, games, and high-quality child care or preschool, as well as parent–child interactions, explain some of the differences between poor and nonpoor children's outcomes (Aber, Bennett, Conley, & Li, 2007). This line of research suggests that owing to the chronic stress of poverty, parents are more likely to display punitive behaviors such as shouting, yelling, and slapping, and less likely to display love and warmth through cuddling and hugging. The struggle of providing for a family with limited financial resources may lead to increased levels of marital conflict, family anxiety, and individual depression, which then im-pair parents' ability to provide a warm, supportive, and enriching atmosphere for their children (Aber et al., 2007).

Although the exact pathways through which poverty influences children's development may not be precisely known, it is likely a combination of factors, in-cluding inadequate nutrition, family stresses that compromise positive, nurturing parenting, reduced early learning opportunities, and lack of high-quality child care. What is clear is that living in poverty puts a child at greater risk for poor health outcomes, reduced cognitive functioning, low academic achievement, so-cioemotional difficulties, and increased risk behaviors such as teen pregnancy, delinquency, and substance abuse (Brooks-Gunn & Duncan, 1997; Pungello, Campbell, & Barnett, 2006). Children from racial/ethnic minority groups, those who have limited English fluency, and children in recent immigrant families are more likely to be growing up in poor households.

Question: Which aspects of poverty do you think are most influential in children's development?

THE IMPORTANCE OF RESILIENCY

Research over the last two decades has consistently shown that most children growing up in deprived and/or highly stressed families manage to respond positively to their life challenges and make decent lives for themselves (Benard, 2004). Beginning with Werner and Smith's (1992) groundbreaking work with a large group of children growing up with risk factors in Hawaii, there is promising research that shows many children in adverse situations are able to develop normally and achieve productive, stable, and satisfying adult lives (Werner & Smith, 2001). This line of research emphasizes the pull toward normal development or self-righting tendencies innate in all of us that is supported by environmental protective factors. Masten (2001) has described resilience as follows: "What began as a quest to understand the extraordinary has revealed the power of the ordinary. Resilience does not come from rare and special qualities, but from the everyday magic of ordinary, normative human resources in the minds, brains, and bodies of children, in their families and relationships, and in their communities" (p. 9).

Resilient children, called "keepers of the dream" by Germezy and Rutter (1983), are children who manage to develop their human potential despite living in chronic poverty or exposure to stressful events. A sense of *self-efficacy* has been identified as one of the key components of resiliency; self-efficacy provides the child with the inner strength to cope successfully with challenges. Rather than behaving as though they are victims of an unfortunate fate, resilient children take an active stance toward achieving important life goals (Rutter, 1984; Werner & Smith, 1989). A resilient child has been described as one who "works well, plays well, loves well, and expects well" (Garmezy, 1974; Werner & Smith, 1989).

Bonnie Benard identified four areas of personal strengths as the manifestations of resiliency: (1) social competence, (2) problem solving, (3) autonomy, and (4) sense of purpose (Benard, 1994). Benard cites other research that suggests these characteristics are both present and important in all cultural groups and across gender (Eccles & Gootman, 2002; Werner & Smith, 2001). These personal strengths that underlie resiliency are viewed as developmental possibilities innate in all individuals that can be fostered through environmental supports and learning opportunities (Benard, 2004). See Table 4.1.

Social competence "includes the qualities of responsiveness, flexibility, empathy and caring, communication skills, a sense of humor, and any other prosocial behavior" (see Table 4.1). Resilient children are considerably more responsive (and can elicit more positive responses from others) than those children who are not. They are also more active, flexible, and adaptable than others, even in infancy (Fraser, 2004; Werner & Smith, 1989). Furthermore, a great number of resilient

TABLE 4.1 Characteristics of Resilient Children

Social Competence	Problem Solving	Autonomy	Sense of Purpose
Responsiveness	Planning	Positive identity	Goal direction, achievement
Communication	Flexibility	Internal locus of control, initiative	Motivation
Empathy/caring	Resourcefulness	Self-efficacy, mastery	Educational aspirations
Compassion	Critical thinking/insight	Adaptive distancing, resistance	Special interest
Altruism		Self-awareness	Creativity imagination
Forgiveness		Mindfulness	Optimism/hope
		Humor	Faith spirituality
			Sense of meaning

Source: From *Resiliency: What We Have Learned*, by B. Benard, 2004, San Francisco, CA: WestEd Publications, p. 14. Copyright 2004 by WestEd Publications. Adapted with permission.

children have a sense of humor; that is, they have the ability to generate comic relief and find alternative ways of looking at things, as well as the ability to laugh at these things and find humor in ridiculous situations (Masten, 2001).

Studies of resilient children have repeatedly found them to possess *problem-solving skills*. Early studies found that preschool children who were able to enact alternatives in frustrating situations went on to have successful grade school experiences (Halverson & Waldron, 1974). In addition, research on street children growing up in the slums of the United States, and children who had been abused and neglected, found that those who could plan and successfully negotiate the demands of their environment were more likely to go on and have healthy adult lives (Felsman, 1989; Rutter, 1984; Segal, 1986).

The ability to *act independently and exert some control* over one's environment has also been identified as a common attribute of resilient children (Garmezy, 1991; Garmezy & Rutter, 1983). Children who are able to maintain an inner locus of control and exert some impulse control in stressful situations were likewise able to achieve constructive goals for themselves. In other words, many resilient children see themselves as capable of acting in their own best interests and not trapped in dysfunctional cycles.

Young children who have a *sense of purpose* and vision of a bright future for themselves are much more likely to achieve positive long-term outcomes (Benard, 2004). This sense of hopefulness, optimism, and high aspirations about the future has been shown to be a powerful predictor of future competence and successful life adaptation. As Marion Wright Edelman, founder of the Children's Defense Fund (CDF) and leader of the CDF adolescent pregnancy prevention initiative, has frequently stated, "[A] bright future is the best contraceptive!" (as cited in Benard, 1994, p. 8).

All young children posses personal strengths and characteristics that should be recognized and celebrated.

These four interrelated domains of strengths seen in all children are especially important for children living in adverse circumstances. Experimental research has demonstrated that children living in poverty who beat the odds and achieve at high levels display many of these personal competencies (Eccles & Gootman, 2002). The childhood environment has successfully engaged some combination of these internal assets that are associated with healthy development. In essence, these children are able to form positive connections with other people, display problem-solving skills, have a strong sense of self and feel a sense of control, and have an orientation toward a bright and compelling future. (For a more detailed discussion of the research on characteristics of resilient children, see Benard, 2004, Chapters 2 and 3.)

WHAT TEACHERS CAN DO

The context and characteristics of a child's environment are critical to the development of these innate strengths; certain characteristics of a child's family, school, and community environment can help to strengthen these personal assets that contribute to resilience in young children living under adverse circumstances. Specifically, early childhood programs can adopt policies and practices promoting these strengths, which have been linked to school achievement and positive long-term outcomes for children living in impoverished homes and communities.

The environmental factors that promote resiliency in children identified in the research include the following:

1. ***Caring and support.*** Researchers have identified a caring and supportive relationship with at least one adult as one of the most important protective factors for resilient children. In fact, Werner (1990) found that a stable and close bond during the first year of life was the most powerful predictor of resiliency in children living in distressed circumstances. Having a warm and

affectionate relationship with at least one adult (not necessarily the mother or father) appears to be a critical protective factor. Werner found "among the most frequently encountered positive role models in the lives of the children of Kauai, outside of the family circle, was a favorite teacher. For the resilient youngster a special teacher was not just an instructor for academic skills, but also a confidant and positive model for personal identification" (1990). For a young child to have a responsive adult care about her and help her feel safe in a dangerous world appears to be an essential aspect of developing personal coping skills. See the following text box for how I personally experienced the power of supportive relationships in the lives of young children with troubling behavior.

2. *Positive expectations.*   Throughout the school improvement and resiliency literature, the value of high expectations is prominent. Schools imparting the message that children are capable and can achieve difficult goals (and provide the support to achieve them) have higher rates of academic success with children from low-income homes than other schools (Education Trust, 2006). When everyone in the program truly believes that *all* children—even those who are poor, those who do not speak English, and those who have

---

Every Child Benefits From One "Special" Person

While I was principal at a prekindergarten through Grade 2 school that served mainly low-income families, most of who were recent immigrants and spoke very little English, I learned the power of positive relationships. As the only on-site administrator, I was responsible for addressing behavior problems and enacting our discipline policies. I often was asked to *straighten out* young 6-, 7-, and 8-year-old children (frequently boys) who had trouble following directions, had trouble sitting through activities, had trouble waiting their turn, or were sometimes physically aggressive to their peers. These youngsters were frustrating their teachers and disrupting the learning in their classrooms.

My first response was always to spend some time getting to know each child. I considered this *golden time*. This was when I found out about their families, their pets, their favorite activities, their best friends, what they liked and disliked about school, and what they were having trouble with. During this time, I also developed a plan of action with each child, detailing the school expectations and the consequences for breaking the rules. Then I set up a schedule that teamed one caring adult, sometimes me but often another staff person, with each child. We found some time each week where we could play a game, take a walk, or just talk with the child.

I discovered that most of these young children who acted out were looking for attention from a caring adult who helped the child feel safe and supported. This combination of individual attention, structured plan of action tailored to each child's identified needs, and schoolwide consistency was most often enough to witness improvements in behavior. In fact, I often saw these difficult-to-manage children become reengaged with school and exert their considerable energies toward creative learning.

While on the playground or during my classroom visits, I deliberately established eye contact, smiled, and acknowledged the child's good work, which helped to affirm our special relationship. Through these positive relationships with mutual regard, I was able to establish a context of trust; I was then able to influence and redirect behavior. My secret to enacting our discipline policies was to work hard on establishing deeper connections and caring relationships.

special needs—have innate talents and are capable of mastering the academic curriculum, more children will be successful.

3. ***Opportunities for meaningful participation.*** Children who actively participate in meaningful ways in their family and school life are more likely to see themselves as worthy and capable of making a positive contribution (Benard, 2004). Werner found that for children growing up in adverse circumstances who were given responsibilities, "such productive roles of responsibility, when associated with close family ties, [were] important protective factors during times of adversity" (1990, p.12). The importance of giving children some degree of responsibility for their own learning is also demonstrated in the High Scope Perry Preschool research (Schweinhart et al., 2005). Minority inner city children from impoverished homes who participated in the High Scope preschool curriculum were much more likely than others of similar backgrounds to finish school, avoid juvenile and adult delinquency, become employed and pay taxes, and generally become stable, productive citizens (Schweinhart et al., 2005). A cornerstone of the High Scope curriculum is the practice of giving preschool children opportunities to plan and execute some portions of their daily schedule (the plan-do-review portion of the day). This practice allows young children to make meaningful decisions about their own learning. See the following text box for another example of how even young children can make contributions to their learning environment.

Young Children Can Make Important Contributions

Experienced teachers will design classroom so that all children can participate in the daily tasks of school life. Children can be assigned roles such as assisting with attendance, noise monitor, weather checker, feeding the plants and animals, classroom host or hostess when parents visit, materials assistance, and so on.

Again, it was during my tenure as a principal in an inner city school where I learned how involving troubled youngsters with important tasks can alter their attitudes toward teachers and school in general. One week our school custodian was unexpectedly absent and the district had no substitutes to send on such short notice. Faced with a play yard that needed to be swept and classrooms that needed to be tidied, I turned to our young "discipline problems." These were youngsters who had often been referred to me because of their disruptive behavior in class.

I called each of them at home and asked their parents if they could come to school a little early and stay a little late for the next week. The next day the children showed up bright and early to find out what I had in store for them. I had organized little brigades with special shirts, brooms, trash cans, and colored bags. To my surprise, each child eagerly accepted his or her assignment and promptly went to work. All day long they kept asking me if they could help me with anything else. Not one of them had any discipline referrals during that week. In fact, they seemed to show a new pride in themselves and their school.

Clearly, I could not continue to assign the children the tasks of cleaning the school; however, I could identify meaningful roles in each classroom and throughout the school that they were capable of carrying out. The beaming sense of pride that these children displayed told me that we all benefit when we feel useful and needed. Young children from highly stressed circumstances may not have any other place where they can demonstrate they are competent and capable. When children are given a responsibility and a meaningful role, they might surprise you with how deeply they respond.

The important message for early childhood educators is that we can deliberately and systematically create programs that foster resiliency in all our children. Many of these program features can and should be integral to program structure and curriculum design for all programs. In all of our educational endeavors, from the daily schedule to the use of discipline, we can incorporate caring and support (e.g., having one staff person assigned to each child who takes the time to develop a close and caring relationship), high expectations (e.g,, consistently communicating to all children that they are capable of doing excellent work and then following through with support), and opportunities for meaningful participation (e.g., letting children contribute to class rules, chores, and choice of activities). Clearly they are essential and attainable components for programs serving children living in low-income households.

Question: How could you incorporate the features of *caring and support, high expectations, and opportunities for meaningful participation* into a preschool program?

SCHOOL READINESS AND LOW-INCOME CHILDREN

A series of reports based on a large national study (Early Childhood Longitudinal Study-kindergarten cohort, ECLS-K) indicates that children from low-income homes enter school lagging behind their more economically advantaged peers in terms of the knowledge and social competencies, which are widely recognized as important for school success. Poverty has been shown to correlate with literacy levels and other indicators of "school readiness" at kindergarten entry (National Center for Educational Statistics, 2003). A national survey has documented that families receiving public assistance have fewer books and recordings in the home. Further, these parents read and tell stories less often to their children (National Center for Educational Statistics, 2003). In fact, high-SES children own about three times as many books as low-SES children; are more likely to visit a public library and own a computer; and have parents who are much more likely to read to them frequently (Lee & Burkham, 2002).

Consequently, children from lower SES families tend to have fewer of the following literacy skills that are prerequisites to learning to read:

- knowing that print reads left to right;
- knowing where to go when a line of print ends;
- knowing where the story ends; and
- having the ability to recognize letters, beginning sounds, and ending sounds of words (Bowman et al., 2000).

Additional research has also revealed that children in lower SES groups have much less verbal interaction with adults than those in higher SES groups, which leads to a much more limited vocabulary (Hart & Risley, 1995, 1999). Children from low-income communities are also much more likely to have difficulty with literacy than low-income children in middle-class or moderate-income communities (Snow, Burns, & Griffin, 1998):

Low SES is an individual risk factor to the extent that among children attending the same schools, youngsters from low-income families are

*more likely to become poor readers than those from high-income fami-
lies. Low SES is a group risk factor because children from low-income
communities are likely to become poorer readers than children from
more affluent communities. Because the former are more likely to attend substandard schools, the correlation between SES and low achievement is probably mediated, in large part, by differences in the quality of
school experiences. (p. 126)*

Many children from poverty backgrounds continue to perform below grade
expectations on core subjects throughout their schooling. For example, national
educational assessments at Grades 8 and 12 show that about 50% of children from
at-risk backgrounds (e.g., low parental education or low family income) score below the "basic" level of reading and math achievement, indicating that they have
less than partial mastery of the knowledge and skills "fundamental for proficient
work" at that grade level (Karoly et al., 2008). In short, substantial numbers of children from low-income families begin kindergarten lagging behind their more affluent peers academically. They remain behind throughout their schooling.

Question: How does growing up in a low-income home relate to other environmental conditions that influence children's school readiness and achievement?

A beacon of hope is the compelling research that has repeatedly shown that
high-quality early education can positively influence the intellectual, academic, and
social development of poor children both immediately and in the long-term. Virtu-
ally all experts in early education and related fields agree that intensive, high-quality
interventions for young children in poverty can have substantial impacts on their future school and life success (Barnett, 2008; Deming, 2008). This line of research has
also demonstrated that to be effective, early childhood programs must provide the
elements of high quality, which include positive relationships, a comprehensive and
coherent curriculum, rich, responsive language interactions, and opportunities for
meaningful parent involvement (Espinosa, 2003; Klein & Knitzer, 2006).

THE IMPORTANCE OF HIGH-QUALITY
CURRICULA: SPECIFIC STRATEGIES

Although the achievement gap at kindergarten entry has been well documented
and linked to poverty, it has also been well established that high-quality early education programs can have large and lasting impacts on the academic achievement
and life adjustments of low-income children (Barnett et al., 2001). Because most of
the gap between low-income and more affluent children is present at kindergarten
entry, it is critically important to enhance learning opportunities prior to formal
schooling. It also appears that young children who are the most vulnerable to
poor developmental outcomes benefit the most from high-quality early intervention (Gormley et al., 2005; Reynolds et al., 2001).

According to a policy brief that I wrote a few years ago (Espinosa, 2003),
high-quality preschools are places where the following occurs:

- ***Children are respected, nurtured, and challenged.*** They enjoy close,
  warm relationships with the adults and other children in their classroom.

They frequently interact and communicate with peers and adults; they do not spend long periods of time waiting, being ignored, or isolated. Children enjoy and look forward to school.

- ***Children have ongoing opportunities to learn important skills, knowledge, and dispositions.*** Classrooms are busy with conversations, projects, experiments, reading, and building activities. The materials and activities are individualized and challenge children's intellectual development. Children do not wander aimlessly and they are not expected to sit quietly for long periods of time.
- ***Children are able to make meaningful decisions throughout the day.*** They can choose from a variety of activities, decide what type of products they want to create, engage in important conversations with friends, and exercise their curiosity.
- ***Children's home language and culture are respected, appreciated, and incorporated into the curriculum and the classroom.***
- ***Children participate in individual, small-group, and large-group activities.*** They learn important social and self-regulation skills through adult guidance and appropriate discipline. Not all children are expected to develop at the same rate; individual needs and abilities are accommodated in all learning activities.
- ***Children learn the skills necessary for future academic success.*** Language and literacy activities include frequent interactive book reading, expanded conversations with adults, opportunities to read and write throughout the day, and a positive, joyful climate for learning. They have opportunities to learn the language of school—how to listen, follow directions, respond to teacher questions, and initiate problem solving.
- ***Children have the opportunity to learn school readiness skills.*** They learn expanded vocabulary, alphabetic principles, phonological awareness; concepts of numbers, shapes, measurement, and spatial relations; task persistence; early scientific thinking; and information about the world and how it works.
- ***Children's natural curiosity is used as a powerful motivator.*** Their interest in everything in their environment as well as ideas and concepts contribute to the design of activities and curriculum.
- ***Children are given variety in their daily schedule.*** A child's day should allow for active and quiet time, indoor and outdoor time, short activities and longer ones to increase attention spans, and careful planning to address all aspects of development for all children (p. 5).

In addition to these child features, high-quality preschools are places where the following take place:

- ***Teachers have, at a minimum, a four-year college degree and specific training in early childhood education.*** They have a deep understanding of child development, teaching methods, and curriculum, allowing them to skillfully promote children's social and cognitive development.
- ***Teachers have frequent, meaningful interactions with children.*** They frequently engage children in meaningful conversation, expand their

knowledge and vocabulary, use open-ended questioning, and encourage problem-solving skills.

- *Teachers teach important concepts such as mathematics and early literacy.* They do this through projects, everyday experiences, collaborative activities, and active curriculum.
- *Teachers regularly assess each child's progress and make adjustments as necessary.* They carefully document the emerging abilities of each child and plan activities that promote increased achievement. They also collaborate with other staff and parents about the meaning of the assessments.
- *Teachers refer children who may have special learning needs for comprehensive evaluation and diagnosis.*
- *Teachers are paid a professional salary with benefits.* All staff are compensated according to their professional preparation, experience, and specialized skills. Career advancement opportunities are available.
- Teachers and other staff are provided with ongoing professional development. There is active supervision, mentoring, and feedback for all staff. There is a climate of trust, respect, and cooperation among all the employees.
- *Teachers communicate respect for the families and warmth for the children.* They are knowledgeable about the languages and cultures of the children and families.
- *Teachers are able to have respectful, collaborative relationships with other staff, parents, and other professionals.* Each classroom has at least one teacher and a second adult who work as a team throughout the day. Standards should reflect, at a minimum, the recommended ratios from the National Association of Education for Young Children for program accreditation. (One staff member to 10 children and group size of no more than 20 for children ages 3 to5.)
- *Teachers use a curriculum with specified goals, approach toward learning, expected outcomes, and assessment procedures.* Teachers should be able to describe their curriculum, why it was chosen, and what they are accomplishing with it.
- *Children have opportunities to learn in spacious, well-equipped classrooms.* These have a variety of age-appropriate materials including art, music, science, language, mathematics, puzzles, dramatic play, and building materials (Espinosa, 2003, p. 6).

Question: How would you describe a high-quality preschool classroom? Which features seem the most important to you?

Research over the past decade affirms these characteristics of quality preschools as being important for *all* children, but they are especially critical for those living in vulnerable circumstances (Klein, & Knitzer, 2006; National Scientific Council on the Developing Child, 2007b; Karoly et al., 2008). In addition, recent research from the Preschool Curriculum Evaluation Report (PCER) has studied the impact of 14 well-designed preschool curriculum models on children's development in five areas: reading, phonological awareness, language, mathematics, and behavior (Institute for Educational Sciences, 2008). According to their analysis, few of the most common preschool curricula had a significant impact on children's performance in the domains assessed at prekindergarten or at the end of kindergarten. What this evaluation tells us is that in average preschool programs that are not part of a national demonstration project, few programs implement a curriculum that has immediate or short-term impacts on skills that have been shown to predict later academic proficiency. There are many aspects of high quality. Focusing on a specific curricular approach may be less important than designing and implementing a comprehensive program that includes child, teacher, and family components.

One of the largest and most influential national programs designed to serve children from low-income homes is Head Start. Head Start was established in 1965 as part of the War on Poverty to provide preschool, health, and other social services to poor children ages 3 to 5 and their families, and currently serves over 900,000 children each year at a cost of around $7 billion (U.S. Department of Health and Human Services, 2009). The mission of Head Start is to bring about a greater degree of social competence in the young children of low-income families. It takes into account the interrelatedness of cognitive and intellectual development, physical and mental health, and nutritional needs. Head Start has been the source of a great deal of research over the five decades since the program's inception. As a federal program focusing on children in the years before formal schooling, most from families with economic, social, health, and/or mental health risk factors, it has served as a national laboratory for implementing and studying a wide range of early childhood program models.

It is difficult to summarize 40 years of research on Head Start's effectiveness, because it is a comprehensive program designed to positively influence children's development, health status, and school readiness as well as overall family functioning. In general, however, the results of the most recent Head Start evaluations show that after one year, Head Start was able to nearly cut in half the achievement gap that would be expected in the absence of the program (U.S. Department of Health and Human Services, 2009). Results also indicate that Head Start has different impacts based on the age of the child and the language spoken in the home. For children in the 3-year-old group whose primary language was English, positive impacts were found on a variety of cognitive outcomes, as well as on particular measures of social-emotional development, health, and parenting practices. Among children in this age group whose primary language was Spanish, impacts were found across several domains, but were fewer in number. For children in the 4-year-old group whose home language was English, positive impacts were found in all domains; for 4-year-old children whose home language was Spanish, impacts were found only in the area of health (U.S. Department of Health and Human Services, 2009). Although most researchers agree that Head Start has positive impacts on important dimensions of school readiness for children from low-income households, there is continuing debate about the cost-effectiveness of such a broad-based approach. Most early childhood advocates agree that some aspects of Head Start need improvement (e.g., teacher qualifications) (Zigler, 2005).

Question: What is the difference between a curriculum and a comprehensive program?

A report by the National Center for Children in Poverty (Klein & Knitzer, 2006) includes a set of recommendations for preschool programs that serve low-income children. They identify two criteria essential for effective preschool curricula (these criteria are based on the National Association for the Education of Young Children [NAEYC] position statement): (1) an intentional curriculum and (2) professional development and effective teacher support.

AN INTENTIONAL CURRICULUM   Effective curricula are based on research and explicitly teach important language/literacy and math skills. C. Copple and S. Bredekamp, in the latest edition of *Developmentally Appropriate Practice in Early Childhood Programs* (Copple & Bredekamp, 2009), state the following: "Whenever you see a great classroom, one in which children are learning and thriving, you can be sure that the teachers (and the administrators who support them) are highly intentional" (p. 33). Teachers have explicit instructional goals for children that guide all aspects of their interactions and classroom planning. Intentional teachers know their children, understand how to promote learning through individualized learning experiences, and reach out to families to support enhanced, enriched, and emotionally nurturing experiences for all children.

The National Early Literacy Panel (NELP) conducted a comprehensive synthesis of the scientific research on the development of literacy skills in young children (National Early Literacy Panel, 2008). This meta-analysis of over 300 peer-reviewed studies identified the following preschool literacy skills as being very important to future reading and writing abilities:

- *Alphabet knowledge.* This is knowing the names and/or sounds of printed letters.
- *Phonological awareness.* This is the ability to detect, manipulate, or analyze component sounds in spoken language, independent of meaning, such as the ability to match similar sounds (i.e., find words that all begin with *m*), and the ability to orally put together two syllables to form a compound word (i.e., "What word do you get when you put *sun* and *shine* together?").
- *Rapid automatized naming of letters/digits.* This is the ability to rapidly name a sequence of repeating random letters, digits, or both.
- *Rapid automatized naming of objects/colors.* This is the ability to rapidly name a sequence of repeating random pictures of familiar objects or colors.
- *Writing/writing name.* This is the ability to write single letters on request or to write one's own name.
- *Phonological memory.* The is the ability to remember spoken information for a short time. In this meta-analysis, rhyming did not turn out to be a good predictor of later literacy abilities.

In addition, NELP studied the impact of different early interventions on these early literacy skills. Essentially, they found that programs explicitly teaching phonological awareness skills combined with print training are effective. This research also found that shared book reading incorporating interactive strategies (e.g., dialogic reading) and rich language interventions promote oral language abilities (National Early Literacy Panel, 2008). An *intentional curriculum* based on current research on early literacy development would include the following strategies:

- *Dialogic reading with individual or small groups of children.* When using this strategy, teachers actively engage children in the process of reading books by the following: asking questions about the objects and pictures in picture books; using "what" and open-ended questions to encourage children to elaborate on their answers; and expanding on the child's response as a way to teach vocabulary and provide more background information (American Library Association, 2004; Arnold & Whitehurst, 1994). Dialogic reading activities need to occur at least 3 times per week and include small groups of children to be effective. Simply reading books to children without including active child participation does not achieve significant effects on children's reading outcomes (Lonigan, 2006).

- *Phonological awareness activities that actively engage children in analysis of words at the syllable or phoneme level with frequent feedback on the child's performance (Yeh, 2003; Yeh & Connell, 2008).* Young children will benefit from learning that when you delete, add, or substitute sounds to words, a new word is formed. They will also learn from frequently playing with the sounds of words. These skills can be taught through a variety of language games that keep the learning process playful and not overly drill-like. For instance, Adams et al. (1998) demonstrated that it is possible to effectively teach phonemic awareness by using listening, clapping syllables, sound–word, and rhyming games. Teachers can promote these skills by the following: learning nursery rhymes and making up their own silly, nonsense rhymes with children; singing songs with small groups of children every day (songs naturally break words into syllables and are a fun way to learn about word sounds); putting two words together to make a new word ("What word would we have if we put *cow* and *boy* together?"); having children change the beginning sounds of their names (i.e., "Jimmy, can you change the /j/ in *Jimmy* to the /t/ sound?" Don't say the letter name, just the sound the letter makes.) The important point is to conduct these literacy activities frequently and to keep them playful.

- *Deliberately and systematically incorporating opportunities for children to learn about the alphabet.* Teachers can take dictation, emphasize letters throughout the day, have children create their own books, use letters and letter sounds in transition activities, and help children learn to write their own names. All of these activities will help preschoolers attend to the shape, sound, and names of letters and capitalize on their intrinsic motivation to communicate through print.

- *Shared book reading with a focus on the print in the book can help preschoolers learn about print knowledge, concepts about print, and early decoding skills.* Teachers can use books of high interest that are culturally appropriate to engage children and demonstrate the salient features of print (e.g., where a word stops and starts, ordering of print from left to right and top to bottom, connecting words to pictures).

PROFESSIONAL DEVELOPMENT
AND EFFECTIVE TEACHER SUPPORTS

The essence of quality in early childhood services is embodied in the expertise and skills of the staff and in their capacity to build positive relationships with young children. The striking shortage of well-trained personnel in the field today indicates that substantial investments in training, recruiting, compensating, and retaining a high quality workforce must be a top priority. National Scientific Council on the Developing Child (2007, p. 4)

The most important ingredient in a high-quality early childhood program is the skill and knowledge of the teacher. More skilled teaching is often associated with greater educational levels and specialized training in child development (Sadowski, 2006). There is a relatively large research base demonstrating that teacher training plays an important role in the kind of interactions and activities young children receive in early childhood programs (Bowman et al., 2001; Focus Council on Early Childhood Education, 2004; National Association for the Education of Young Children, 2001). In other words, all teachers can continually improve their professional skills through a commitment to lifelong learning. No matter what formal degree a person attains, that person can always refine his or her knowledge and skills based on new research and knowledge. The critical role of the teacher, combined with increasing knowledge about the core knowledge essential for effective early childhood teaching (Sadowski, 2006), has led to the following recommendations for ECE professional development.

- ***Teachers in effective programs need to have educational preparation and specialized training in early childhood.*** Although findings of studies on early education and teacher education have been somewhat mixed, most have found a relationship between quality of educational experiences in the preschool classroom and teachers who have at least a bachelor's degree and specialized training in early childhood (Early et al., 2006; Pianta et al., 2007; Whitebook, 2003). The research cannot tell us yet the exact number and types of courses that an effective early childhood teacher must take or how much difference a bachelor's degree makes, but it is clear that all early educators need to be knowledgeable about the following:
  - child development,
  - curriculum design,
  - specific methods for teaching diverse children,
  - multiple assessment approaches,
  - organization of learning environments,
  - professional collaboration,
  - working with families; and
  - how to reflect on their practices with colleagues and mentors so they can continually improve (Klein & Knitzer, 2006; Sadowski, 2006).
- ***All teachers working with low-income young children need ongoing professional development and classroom support to skillfully implement the practices described in this volume.*** Knowledge of a child's

Early childhood teachers and support staff enjoy opportunities to learn new teaching strategies.

ability, background, and needs, combined with a deep understanding of the curriculum goals and recommended instructional strategies, requires that teachers engage in systematic personal and professional development. Knowing the instructional strategies is one thing, knowing how to apply them with a specific child under particular conditions to achieve important goals is quite another. The following professional development practices have been identified as helping to improve the quality of early learning:

- individualized classroom coaching and mentoring;
- one-to-one consultation;
- carefully sequenced and ongoing workshops;
- using interactive media to promote deeper understanding of development; and
- continuous progress monitoring (Brandon et al., 2006; Pianta, 2003; Preston et al., 2005).

Question: As a beginning teacher, what types of professional development and classroom support would you like to have available to you? What types of professional development do you think are most beneficial to experienced teachers?

ACHIEVING SUCCESS: SCHOOLS, FAMILIES, AND COMMUNITIES WORKING TOGETHER

Through a careful synthesis of research from a variety of disciplines, it is possible to create a comprehensive approach to early education for children living in poverty. We have good information from neurobiology, developmental psychology, educational evaluations, and cognitive and medical science that offers related perspectives on the components of high-quality early education for low-income children. The National Scientific Council on the Developing Child (2007b, p. 2) has recently stated the following:

> *The need to address significant inequalities in opportunity, beginning in the earliest years of life, is both a fundamental moral responsibility and a critical investment in our nation's social and economic future. Thus, the time has come to close the gap between what we know (from systematic scientific inquiry across a broad range of disciplines) and what we do (through both public and private sector policies and practices) to promote the healthy development of all young children. The science of early childhood development can provide a powerful framework for informing sound choices among alternative priorities and for building consensus around a shared plan of action. The well being of our nation's children and the security of its future would be well served by such wise choices and concerted commitment.*

It is clear that young children living in poverty often do not receive the early education that is so critically important to their future success. Many either are not enrolled in any program or attend programs judged to be of lower quality. This represents a needless waste of human potential as well as an abandonment of our collective moral responsibility. The most effective programs targeting low-income children have emphasized the importance of developing close partnerships with parents and involving the broader community in program activities (Ramey & Ramey, 1989; Reynolds, 2007; Schweinhart et al., 2005). As Art Reynolds, the lead researcher of the Child-Parent Centers in the Chicago Public Schools has said, "The program is an outreach to the parents as well. . . . In order to lift families out of poverty, attention is directed to the whole family" (2007, p. 1).

The current research on parent involvement programs strongly suggests that to be effective with nontraditional families, programs need to expand beyond the "compliance model" of parent involvement in which parents receive information from teachers and are expected to carry out teachers' requests (Taylor, 1991). These programs need to embrace a more reciprocal learning model (Compton-Lilly & Comber, 2003). In the reciprocal learning model, both parents and teachers are viewed as givers and receivers of important information (Paratore, 2005). In successful programs that engage parents living in distressed circumstances, researchers have pointed to the need to emphasize practices that help build partnerships and to avoid a one-size-fits-all approach (Paratore, 2005).

Joyce Epstein has identified the following six types of parent involvement (Epstein et al., 2002). In Epstein's model, parents and schools share overlapping *spheres of influence.*

Type 1: *Parenting*
Assist families with parenting skills and setting home conditions to support children as students. Also, assist schools to better understand families.

Type 2: *Communicating*
Conduct effective communications from school-to-home and from home-to-school about school programs and student progress.

Type 3: *Volunteering*
Organize volunteers and audiences to support the school and students. Provide volunteer opportunities in various locations and at various times.

Type 4: *Learning at Home*
Involve families with their children on homework and other curriculum-related activities and decisions.

Type 5: *Decision Making*
Include families as participants in school decisions, and develop parent leaders and representatives.

Type 6: *Collaborating with the Community*
Coordinate resources and services from the community for families, students, and the school, and provide services to the community.

When parents and schools form partnerships, all children benefit from the connected and caring community formed around them. The reciprocal influences of school and family help schools become more family-like and families become more school-like. In a sense, each entity helps to reinforce the function of the other. Family-like schools welcome all families and recognize the unique and special qualities of each child, while school-like families help to extend the classroom learning into the home and support the academic skills that will ensure future school success. Within this framework, each program will look different, but all will employ a variety of types of involvement, depending on the specific conditions present in each community and family. Not all parents will be able to engage in all six types of involvement, but all parents can engage in some type of partnership activity.

The different types of involvement each generate a variety of practices that will have benefits for children, parents, and teachers. The point for early childhood educators is that parents can be actively engaged with the school at many different levels, any one of which can be effective and beneficial, depending on the family and school circumstances. (For a more detailed description of parent involvement practices, see Epstein et al., 2002, pp. 13–17.)

Question: Which types of parent involvement are you most familiar with? Which types do you think are most common in schools?

Although it has been shown that excellent teachers in quality programs can help to override less than ideal home conditions, it has also been suggested that "in the absence of excellence in the classroom, the role of the home becomes much more important" (Snow et al., 1991, p. 161). We also have strong evidence that "parents with low income and less formal education, who may have weaker reading skills than more economically advantaged parents, can effectively support their children's reading and education" (Sheldon & Epstein, 2005, p. 113). Because we know that many low-income children are not receiving high-quality education from well-prepared teachers, we urgently need to provide guidance on *which* family involvement approaches are best suited to *which* groups of parents.

In particular, Moll, Armanti, Neff, and Gonzalez(1992) have argued for incorporating family and community resources in classrooms to make school more meaningful for low-income and minority children. The funds of knowledge that are available in children's families and communities represent rich intellectual and social resources for children that are culturally relevant. By incorporating what families know, what they value, and how they communicate their cultural knowledge, programs can increase home–school congruence and build on what young children already know.

All families have some special interest or talent that can be brought into the classroom. For example, in one prekindergarten program that I administered, the parents were reluctant to become involved in the school activities and meetings because of their poor English skills. Once the school staff discovered that many of the families had small gardens and took great pride in their fresh vegetables, we asked if they could help us plant a garden for the children in our empty school plot. This seemed to energize many formerly distant mothers and fathers. They started showing up on Monday morning to demonstrate to the children how to dig up the soil, the correct depth to plant each type of seed, and how much water to use for each plant. We all learned and grew from these garden days: rich science and vocabulary lessons were planned around the garden; parents, children, and teachers developed new connections and skills; and our whole school gained respect for the specialized talents of our families.

COMPREHENSIVE SUPPORT FOR FAMILIES Children from low-income homes are more likely to have health and behavioral problems at kindergarten entry (Golan, Spiker, & Sumi, 2005). Good health has been repeatedly linked to better school performance and better transitions to kindergarten (Golan et al., 2005; NSCDC, 2007c). Based on these and other reports, First 5, a California-based initiative designed to provide an integrated system of early childhood services, has recommended that all early childhood programs provide parenting education and support services (First 5, 2007). Families that participated in parenting education classes and received support services were more likely to ensure that their children participated in developmental screenings and received regular medical checkups. Specifically, they have recommended the following community-based practices to support healthy child development and school readiness:

1. Support family literacy and parenting education programs that encourage parents to read to and interact with their children in ways that help their development. Family support and education services are critical for ensuring that children are ready to succeed in school when they enter kindergarten. These programs can affect home literacy, health care access, receipt of developmental screenings, and enrollment in high-quality preschool programs— all-important predictors of school readiness.
2. Conduct developmental screenings, so that children with special needs can be identified early and receive critical services before they enter kindergarten.

3. Provide young children with high-quality early childhood education programs. School readiness initiative programs also support high-quality preschools by providing training to preschool staff on best teaching practices and by funding expansions of existing preschool programs.

4. Develop health insurance enrollment programs; oral health treatment, screening, and prevention services; and nutrition education and assessments.

5. Connect families to important community resources and services.

6. Tailor services to better meet the needs of the families who can most benefit from them. Programs need to be accessible to families who speak Spanish and other languages other than English; they also need to use strategies that build the literacy skills of parents and address the needs of children of various ages. For example, many programs can provide or partner with other programs that provide remedial or secondary education, adult literacy classes, and classes in English as a second language (Golan et al., 2005).

It is apparent that all parents have goals and aspirations for their children—even parents who are struggling in economically distressed circumstances. These parental goals have been linked to children's school readiness in samples of Head Start children (Bettler & Burns, 2003). What parents value most dearly and the dreams they have for their children can be used to build bridges between family culture and school curriculum. When parents say they want their children to be well behaved and respectful to adults, educators can use this language to design curriculum that addresses both home and school goals. By starting where the parents are and using the language of the home, schools will improve their ability to form strong partnerships with families who in other circumstances might be labeled "hard to reach."

Summary

Decades of scientific studies have demonstrated that poverty can have a substantial and adverse influence on children's overall development. Certain groups are more likely to experience poverty and its corresponding negative consequences: African Americans, Latinos, American Indians, recent immigrants, single parents, and households with low levels of parental education. Although poverty, in and of itself, is a risk factor for depressed development—particularly chronic poverty—there is reason to believe that well-designed, high-quality early education can improve the life chances of children growing up in adverse circumstances.

Early childhood programs can systematically promote resiliency in all children.

The characteristics found in resilient children—social competence, problem solving, autonomy, and a sense of purpose—comprise a central core of personal strength that helps steer children toward positive development. These personal strengths can be fostered in all ECE programs and extended to families and communities.

We now have reliable information about the essential elements of high-quality early childhood programs that have proven to enhance the learning trajectories of children living in distressed circumstances. We know how to promote important language and literacy outcomes, how to design intentional curricula, and how to engage parents in meaningful partnerships. Early childhood educators cannot change the economic realities of the children and families we serve, but we can use the available science to improve the conditions of schooling. All of this converging knowledge leads us to educational and ethical obligations; it is time to put into practice what we know.

Reflection and Discussion Questions

1. Think of a child you know who is living in "less than ideal circumstances." What do you see as the child's sources of resilience, the individual strengths the child demonstrates, and the factors that promote resilience in his or her environment?
2. How are you promoting resilience within your family, classroom, and community?
3. Which features of high quality do you implement regularly (or have you observed in classrooms)? How are you addressing the language and literacy needs of all children and/or students?
4. Which strategies have you found effective when working with families?

Research on the Development, Learning, and Teaching of Young English Language Learners

Assumptions underlying the National Panel on Language—Minority Children and Youth: (a) all children in the United States should be able to function fully in the English language; (b) English language learners should be held to the same expectations and have the same opportunities for achievement in academic content areas as other students; and (c) in an increasingly global economic and political world, proficiencies in languages other than English and an understanding of different cultures are valuable in their own right and represent a worthwhile goal for schools.

AUGUST & SHANAHAN, 2008, P. 6

As discussed in Chapter 2, early childhood educators increasingly will be working with children and families from diverse ethnic, cultural, and linguistic backgrounds. There is no question that all of us need to develop the skills, knowledge, and most importantly, the dispositions and attitudes to effectively teach in multicultural and multilingual settings. This is no easy task, because it is a great challenge to understand and correctly interpret the intentions and behaviors of children being raised in households that may not share the prevailing culture's values, customs, language, and/or norms for communicating. However, because children from different cultures who enter school programs speaking little or no English are among the most vulnerable to chronic academic underachievement and eventual school failure, all early childhood educators need to develop strategies to support the developmental, linguistic, and academic success of *all* learners, including English language learners.

As the following example illustrates, teachers can make the difference between success and failure. This scenario is about a Cuban immigrant who entered first grade knowing no English. The school had no bilingual program for him.

Unintelligible noise is all that my cousin and I heard when we first heard English spoken to us. We clung together as we approached our school on the first day. I knew that we would be all right as long as we stayed together. It never occurred to me that we would be separated and placed in different classes. Once I got over my terror at this event, I saw the friendly face of a person who held my hand and comforted me. She was my new teacher. She smiled and stayed close to me, making me feel more secure.

My teacher taught me English when she could fit it into the day, sometimes over lunch. She taught me words in English and asked me to teach her words in Spanish. Once she learned some words and phrases, she taught them to the rest of the class. My new friends knew colors and how to count in Spanish, as well as basic greetings. They even learned my favorite song, "Los Pollitos." I would recite what I had learned in English and my classmates would clap for me. Sometimes we would get extra time at recess or a special activity because I had learned so many words in English and had taught my classmates and teacher so much Spanish.

My cousin had a very different experience. His teacher did not understand him, laughed at mispronounced words, and would not "listen" to him unless he spoke in complete sentences. He became angry and ashamed. He was sometimes punished for refusing to speak. Eventually he refused to cooperate on anything.

My cousin hated school and I loved it. At the end of first grade, I was promoted to second grade while my cousin failed his first year and had to repeat first grade with the same teacher. (as cited in Alvarez et al., 1992, p. 3)

ISSUES AND CONSIDERATIONS FOR YOUNG ELLs

The increasing numbers of young children who are not systematically introduced to English until they enter preschool and rising rates of immigration across the country means that preschool programs and teachers must decide on policies and teaching practices for young children whose first language is not English (see the following definition on next page). This issue has become especially urgent because of the growing trend to test children in English at kindergarten entry. The accountability requirements of the No Child Left Behind Act also directs public schools to test the English proficiency of all ELLs annually. In addition, many school districts require English academic testing at kindergarten entry to assess the effectiveness of their prekindergarten programs (such as the Florida kindergarten screening program).

> ### Defining English Language Learners/Dual Language Learners
>
> Children whose first language is not English are often referred to as *English language learners* (ELLs). This definition includes those learning English for the first time in the preschool setting, as well as children who have developed various levels of English proficiency. Some states, e.g., California, use the term *English learners* (ELs).
>
> Young English learners are increasingly being referred to as *dual language learners*. A recent federal report defines dual language learners as young children, between 3 and 6 years of age, who are learning a second language while still developing basic competency in their first language (Ballantyne, Sanderman, D'Emilio, & McLaughlin, 2008).

Thus, many preschool programs feel pressure to promote rapid English acquisition without any clear guidance on the methods to achieve English fluency or how to deal with the child's home language. In addition, some states (i.e., California and Massachusetts) have passed English-only legislation that mandates the rapid transition to English in the K–12 program with almost no attention to promoting or supporting the child's home language. These issues lead to the following questions that need to be answered by each program as it designs appropriate curriculum, teaching strategies, and assessment approaches for young ELLs:

- What are the goals for ELL children: bilingualism, biliteracy, English only? How do these goals relate to language goals for all the children?
- How do young children learn a second language?
- What is the role of home language development in English acquisition and what happens to children when they lose their home language?
- Is it possible to use both home language and English without confusing the children and delaying the acquisition of English?
- What specific teaching strategies should be used to achieve the language goals for ELL children?
- What assessment procedures should be used? How do we know if ELL children are successfully maintaining their home language and making progress in English acquisition? How do these benchmarks differ from monolingual English speakers?
- What are the resources necessary to achieve our goals for ELL children?

To fairly answer these questions, program staff and administrators need to be familiar with the most current research and carefully consider how these scientific findings can be best applied to their particular set of circumstances. The following sections will present research findings that help to answer these questions and offer recommendations for early childhood teachers and programs.

> *Myth*
> ✓ An unfounded or false notion or belief.
> ✓ Popular belief or legend that has grown up around something or someone; a legend, usually made up in part of historical events, that helps define the beliefs of a people.

Myths About ELLs

I recently wrote a policy brief that challenged some common beliefs about dual language learners based on the current scientific evidence (Espinosa, 2008b). The following six myths about teaching ELLs are simply that: myths. (See definition of myth in above text box.) They are beliefs not supported by research evidence from developmental psychology, neuroscience, psycholinguistics, and/or educational evaluation studies.

1. Learning two languages during the early childhood years will overwhelm, confuse, and/or delay a child's acquisition of English.
2. Total English immersion from prekindergarten through third grade is the best way for a young ELL to acquire English.
3. Because schools often do not have the capacity to provide instruction in all of the languages represented by the children, they should provide English-only instruction.
4. Native English speakers will experience academic and language delays if they are enrolled in dual language programs.
5. Spanish-speaking Latinos show social as well as academic delays when entering kindergarten.
6. Latino ELLs are less likely to be enrolled in prekindergarten programs, because of their families' cultural values (Espinosa, 2008b).

The subsequent sections will review the current research evidence and offer recommendations about teaching strategies based on what we know about the learning and development of young ELL children.

Question: Which of the six myths described earlier about teaching ELLs seems most contrary to what you have previously understood about young children and bilingualism?

ELLs AND SCHOOL READINESS: OVERLAPPING INFLUENCES OF LANGUAGE AND POVERTY

The extent of the child's school "readiness" as assessed at kindergarten entry almost always includes some measure of language abilities. Two large national studies of children's language abilities prior to kindergarten entry—the ECLS-K cohort and the Head Start National Reporting System (NRS)—have shed light on ELL early language development. In both studies, all children were assessed in certain aspects of their language development in English. If the child did not pass a short English language screener and spoke Spanish at home, the child was then assessed in Spanish. No other home languages were assessed in these large national studies. In the ECLS-K, the child's Spanish fluency was assessed at only one point in time. On the other hand, in the NRS (which was a biannual standardized assessment in Head Start that has been discontinued), if Spanish was the language of assessment at the initial fall testing, the child was assessed in Spanish and English during the spring testing (Office of Head Start, 2008).

Analysis of these two national data sets reveals that young Latino ELLs at school entry are more likely to live in low-income homes (Espinosa et al., 2006a), live with both parents, and have a mother who is less likely to work outside the home than their White or African American peers (Crosnoe, 2004). Low-income Hispanic children in the ECLS-K sample also scored more than half a standard deviation below the national average in math and reading achievement at kindergarten entry. This means they are functioning at six months to one year below their middle-class peers (Lee & Burkham, 2002). These achievement disparities persist as children who are not native English speakers continue to have substantially lower levels of educational achievement, including high school completion and college enrollment rates, than their peers from English-only backgrounds (Gandara, Rumberger, Maxwell-Jolly, & Callahan 2003; Rumberger & Anguiano, 2004).

When the data from this large national study are broken down according to which language is spoken in the home (English, European—languages spoken in Europe other than English or Spanish—Asian, or Spanish) and the SES of the home, the discrepancies in the initial achievement scores as well as the amount of growth over time are greatly reduced (Espinosa et al., 2006a). The ELL children from households speaking European or Asian languages were much less likely to live in low socioeconomic homes and had school achievement scores that were comparable to and in some cases exceeded their English-speaking peers. Children from Spanish-speaking homes who did not meet basic English proficiency levels at initial testing were overwhelmingly in the lowest SES groups (80%).

> *These are children who do not have basic fluency in English, speak mostly Spanish in the home, and are living in poor or near poor households. While this analysis did not ask about their fluency in Spanish, their home language, that is one of the questions that needs to be asked. We know that these children are living in reduced economic circumstances and have not mastered simple English vocabulary; we do not know the level of their first language development. (Espinosa et al., 2006a, p. 49)*

In addition, this analysis of the ECLS-K data set by language type revealed that when compared as a group, the ELL children scored below their native English-speaking peers on math and reading assessments, but when compared by language type, the findings were more nuanced. "In general, . . . children from European and Asian speaking homes do as well or better than their English speaking counterparts. Children from Spanish speaking homes are behind all other language groups. The difference is pronounced when the achievement scores of the Spanish speaking children who score lower than the cutoff are compared to the English speaking children or to the Spanish speaking children who score above the cutoff score" (Espinosa et al., 2006a, p. 52). However, as a national report has recently pointed out,

> *The major reason why levels of school readiness and school achievement are lower for Hispanic children than for Whites is that a high percentage of Hispanic youngsters are from low socioeconomic status (SES) families—families in which the parents have little formal education and low incomes. (National Task Force on Early Childhood Education for Hispanics, 2007, p. 1)*

Clearly, the economic and educational resources of the family influence the child's academic knowledge at kindergarten entry. The finding that the vast majority of the children who had limited English fluency and spoke Spanish at home were also living in reduced economic circumstances leads to a question about their native language fluency. That is, how fluent were they in their home language? Were they as fluent as their peers who have other home languages, such as English, Asian languages, and European languages? Based on other research of the language-learning opportunities and overall language development of children living in poverty discussed in Chapter 4, it is quite possible that these Spanish-speaking children are also behind in their native language abilities. The research available suggests that the long-term achievement of ELL children is influenced greatly by the circumstances of their early learning environment not just the fact that they are dual language learners. Others have concluded that, *all things being equal, children have no difficulty acquiring two languages during the preschool years—and will benefit from becoming bilingual* (Genesee et al., 2004). All things, however, are rarely equal!

Implications for Teachers

Thus, it is important to remember that there is great diversity within our ELL population. They vary in the following characteristics:

- the home language they speak,
- the age at which they were first exposed to English,
- their fluency in both their first language and English, and
- in the level of family and community resources available to support their overall language development.

These economic, linguistic, and cultural differences are significant and should not be overlooked. ELL children and families should not all be lumped together and treated as though they share the same strengths and needs. Each child and family needs to be approached as individuals.

Nevertheless, by the common standards through which we measure educational success—math and reading standardized achievement test scores, high school completion rates, higher education enrollment, and English language proficiency—Latino ELLs as a group are behind even before they reach the starting line of formal schooling.

The important consideration for educators and policy makers in this climate of accountability and high-stakes testing is the role of language and culture in school success. Is a child from a Mexican American immigrant family that speaks Spanish in the home necessarily "at risk" for school failure? What are the talents, resources, and strengths of this young child and her family? How can the early education program recognize, support, and expand the *funds of knowledge* (Gonzalez, Moll, & Amanti, 2005) that young Latinos bring into the school?

LOOK FOR FUNDS OF KNOWLEDGE   Luis Moll and his colleagues have demonstrated through first-hand research with families how the life experiences of all children have given them *funds of knowledge* (Moll et al., 1992). Funds of knowledge refers to those family customs (e.g., skills, abilities, ideas, practices) or bodies of knowledge that have developed over time and contribute to a family's well-being and functioning. By taking the time to visit the homes of families, teachers can observe firsthand each family's existing knowledge and cultural strengths.

A fund of knowledge can be something as simple as extensive gardening expertise or as complex as knowing all about animal husbandry. Within this framework, all families have strengths and resources that have allowed them to construct knowledge in their everyday practices and interactions. According to this perspective, schools have an obligation to link their instruction to the community contexts and local family histories. By tapping into the rich funds of knowledge present in children's households and communities, teachers can design curriculum that reflects and capitalizes on children's existing knowledge. The culturally embedded knowledge of the home is confirmed and respected while extended into academically relevant and challenging goals. According to Cummins (1994), teacher–child interactions that build on children's cultural knowledge and strengths are central to positive self-images of language minority children.

ROLE OF HOME LANGUAGE IN ENGLISH ACQUISITION

When young children growing up in a home that speaks a language other than English enter an early childhood program, it is important to remember that they already know much about language—how to use it, lots of vocabulary words, how to construct meaning—but they don't know the specific features of the English language. When we think about how to introduce English, how to recognize and incorporate each child's existing knowledge, and what rate of progress we should expect, it is important to understand the process of dual language development. Research increasingly shows that most young children are capable of learning two languages and that bilingualism confers cognitive, cultural, and economic advantages (Bialystok, 2001; Genesee et al., 2004; Hakuta & Pease-Alvarez, 1992). Bilingualism has been associated with a greater awareness of and sensitivity to linguistic structure, an awareness transferred and generalized to certain early literacy and nonverbal skills.

The recent research on the impact of learning two languages during the infant–toddler years has also highlighted the extensive capacity of the human brain to learn multiple languages, the ability of the infant to separate out each language and interpret context cues to know when it is appropriate to use which language (Kuhl, 2004). For example, preschool-aged children who are learning both English and Spanish have demonstrated the ability to use the appropriate language in conversation, depending on the language ability of the partner (Genesee et al., 2004). In addition, these studies have demonstrated that knowing more than one language does not delay the acquisition of English or impede academic achievement in English when both languages are supported and learned before the age of 7. As stated recently,

> *There is wide scientific consensus that bilingual infants develop two separate but connected linguistic systems during the first year of life. We now know that infants have the innate capacity to learn two languages from birth and that this early dual language exposure does not delay development in either language. (Espinosa, 2008b, p. 4)*

HOW DO YOUNG CHILDREN LEARN A SECOND LANGUAGE?

Many parents and educators assume that preschool-aged children can just "pick up" a second language without systematic teaching, simply with enough exposure. However, becoming proficient in a language is a complex and demanding process that takes many years. As with any type of learning, children will vary enormously in the rate at which they learn a first and a second language. The speed of language acquisition is attributable to factors both within the child and in the child's learning environment. The child's personality, aptitude for languages, interest, and motivation to learn a second language all interact with the quantity and quality of language inputs to influence the rate and eventual fluency levels.

SIMULTANEOUS VERSUS SEQUENTIAL SECOND LANGUAGE ACQUISITION   Barry McLaughlin (1984, 1995) has made a distinction between children who learn a second language *simultaneously* or *sequentially/successively*. When a child learns two languages *simultaneously* during the earliest stages of language development, the developmental pathway is similar to how monolingual children acquire language. Their development of vocabulary, grammar, and early literacy skills occurs at roughly the same time as monolingual children. In fact, the majority of young children in the world successfully learn two languages (or more) from the first years of life (Reyes & Moll, 2006). However, there is evidence that when young children are learning two languages, the rate of vocabulary development may be very different in each language than the typical rate for monolingual children. As children are acquiring two languages and becoming bilingual, one language may dominate, depending on the child's exposure to each language. The ELL child's dominant language may also change during the preschool years. That is normal (Espinosa, 2007b).

The language development of children who learn a second language after the first language is established (usually defined as after 3 years of age), or *sequentially*, follows a different progression and is highly sensitive to characteristics of the child as well as the language-learning environment. At this point, the basics of the child's first language have been learned. They know how their first language works, but now must learn the specific features—grammar, vocabulary, and syntax—of a new language. According to Tabors and Snow (1994), *sequential* or *successive* second language acquisition follows a four-stage developmental sequence:

1. *Home language use.* When a child has become competent in one language and is introduced into a setting where everyone is speaking a different language (e.g., an ELL child entering an English-dominant preschool classroom), the child will frequently continue to speak his home language even when others do not understand. This period can be as short as a few days; in some cases, the child will persist in trying to get others to understand him for months.

2. *Nonverbal/observational period.* After young children realize that speaking their home language will not work, they enter a period where they rarely speak and use nonverbal means to communicate. This is a period of active language learning for the child; he is busy listening to and learning the features, sounds, and words of the new language (receptive language), but not yet verbally using the new language to communicate. This is an extremely important stage of second language learning that, again, may last a long time or be brief. Any language assessments conducted during this stage of development

may result in misleading information that underestimates the child's true language capacity.

3. ***Telegraphic and formulaic speech.*** The child is now ready to start using the new language and does so through telegraphic speech that involves the use of formulas. This is similar to a monolingual child who is learning simple words or phrases (content words) to express whole thoughts. For instance, a child might say, "Me down," indicating he wants to go downstairs. Formulaic speech refers to unanalyzed chunks of words or sometimes even syllables strung together that are repetitions of what the child has heard. For example, Tabors (1997/2008) reports that ELLs in the preschool she studied frequently used the phrase "Lookit" to engage others in their play. These are phrases the children had heard from others that helped to achieve their social goals, even though the children probably did not know the meaning of the two words and were only repeating familiar sounds that were functionally effective.

4. ***Productive language.*** Now the child is starting to go beyond telegraphic or formulaic utterances to create his own phrases and thoughts. Initially the child may use very simple grammatical patterns such as "I wanna play," but over time he will gain control over the structure and vocabulary of the new language. Errors in language use are common during this period as children are experimenting with their new language and learning its rules and structure.

As with any developmental sequence, the stages are flexible and not mutually exclusive. McLaughlin and his colleagues (McLaughlin, Blanchard, & Osanai, 1995) preferred to describe the process as waves, "moving in and out, generally moving in one direction, but receding, then moving forward again" (pp. 3–4).

Young ELLs benefit from vocabulary instruction in both languages.

Sequential bilingual children may have somewhat different patterns of development than monolinguals in certain aspects of language development in the short-term (Espinosa & Lopez, 2007). This may include vocabulary, early literacy skills, and interpersonal communication. Young sequential ELLs frequently know fewer vocabulary words in both English and their home language than monolingual children. This may be caused by the limited memory capacity of young children (developmental), or limited exposure to a rich and varied vocabulary (environmental), or some combination of the two. If the child speaks one language in the home and is learning English at preschool, she may also know some words in one language and not the other. For instance, the child may have learned the English words *recess, chalk, line,* and so on at school, but never learned the corresponding words in Spanish because there was no need or opportunity to do so in the home. However, when the total number of words the child knows in both languages is considered together, most often it is comparable to the number and range of vocabulary words that monolingual children know. Nevertheless, when young ELL children are growing up in environments that have limited language-learning opportunities, their vocabulary knowledge in each language often appears delayed.

CODE SWITCHING/LANGUAGE MIXING   It is important for early childhood educators to understand that *code switching* (switching languages for portions of a sentence) and *language mixing* (inserting single items from one language into another) are normal aspects of second language acquisition. For instance, a young Spanish speaker may say, "He is *pegging* me." The child does not know the English word *hit*, so he substitutes the Spanish word *pegar*, then adds the *ing* ending. Or a very young Spanish speaker may say, "I want more *leche* [milk]."

This does not mean that the child is confused or cannot separate the languages. The main reason that children mix the two languages in one communication is because they lack sufficient vocabulary in one or both languages to fully express themselves. Research has shown that even proficient adult bilinguals mix their languages to convey special emphasis or establish cultural identity (Garcia, 2003). In any case, code switching or language mixing is a normal and natural part of second language acquisition that parents and teachers should not be concerned about. The goal must always be on enhancing communication, rather than enforcing rigid rules about which language can be used at a given time or under certain circumstances.

Young children who have regular and rich exposure to two languages during the early childhood years can successfully become bilingual. Most research concludes that with sufficient input there are no negative effects of bilingualism on the linguistic, cognitive, or social development of children. There may even be some general advantages in these areas of development (Bialystok, 2002; Genesee et al., 2004). Simultaneous bilingualism follows a path similar to monolingual development; sequential second language acquisition occurs in a predictable series of stages or waves. Typically, at any given time, one language may dominate, depending on the amount of time spent in each language. As early childhood programs become increasingly diverse, teachers will need to understand the process of second language acquisition and how to adapt their expectations and instruction accordingly.

Increased understanding will lead to improved methods that will promote the learning and achievement of young children learning English as a second language.

Early childhood educators are often concerned about the rates at which ELL children are acquiring English. It may seem that some of the children who do not speak English at home are learning quite rapidly, while others continue to struggle and avoid using the new language. It is important to remember that all ELL children are unique developmentally and in the language-learning opportunities they have. There is growing research on the factors that influence how rapidly ELL children become proficient in English.

RATE OF ENGLISH ACQUISITION   Young children who successfully learn English seem to possess certain social skills (Wong Fillmore, 1976, 1979; Valdés, 1986). These social abilities appear to affect the rate at which preschool-aged children acquire English:

1. Join groups and pretend to understand what is going on even if you do not; this is the "fake it till you make it" approach toward communicating in a new language.
2. Use the limited language ability you have to give the impression that you can speak English. This will motivate other children to continue to interact with you.
3. Find friends who will help you learn English. The English-speaking friend will provide opportunities to practice the new language as well as the social motivation to keep trying.

Social confidence, an outgoing personality, and the willingness to take risks all appear to facilitate a young child's rapid English acquisition in a preschool setting (Tabors, 1997/2008). A child's *language aptitude* also influences the ease with which children (and adults) successfully learn languages. *Language aptitude* refers to a specific ability that is distinct from general intelligence and includes skills such as the "ability to rapidly and accurately decode unfamiliar speech into phonetic (sound) units and parts of speech (e.g., nouns, verbs, adjectives). It is considered an intrinsic, not a learned, skill. Language aptitude is much more explanatory of individual differences in adult learners than personality and social style variables and may be a relevant factor in explaining why some Language minority children acquire English faster than others" (Genesee et al., 2004, p. 139).

It seems that it is possible to encourage certain social skills and arrange early educational settings that will promote rapid English acquisition. However, as we engage in these practices, we also must ask, Does this put the continued development of the home language at risk? What are the consequences on a child's social development of learning English while losing the ability to communicate in the home language?

LOSS OF HOME LANGUAGE   When preschool children learn two languages, they are learning two cultures. For Latino children who speak Spanish in the home, the second language they learn, English, is the dominant, mainstream language and corresponds to the more powerful White culture that is evident in U.S. classrooms. Many researchers have documented the fragility of a child's home language and cultural practices when they are not highly valued or mainstream. Genesee et al. (2004) have cautioned that "dual language children are particularly at risk for both cultural and linguistic identity displacement" *(p. 33).*

They further argue the following:

> *Erasing a child's language or cultural patterns of language use is a great loss for the child. Children's identities and senses of self are inextricably linked to the language they speak and the culture to which they have been socialized. They are, even at an early age, speakers of their languages and members of their cultures. Language and culture are essential to children's identities. All of the affectionate talk and interpersonal communication of their childhoods and family life are embedded in their languages and cultures. (p. 33)*

Other researchers have linked loss of home language with poor long-term academic outcomes (Slavin & Cheung, 2005; Oller & Eilers, 2002). Slavin and Cheung (2005) reviewed all the experimental studies on reading instruction for ELLs and concluded that teaching reading in the child's home language and English at different times of the day leads to the best reading outcomes. They go on to explain why this may be a resolution to the bilingual debate: "Proponents of bilingual education want to launch English language learners with success while maintaining and valuing the language they speak at home. Opponents are concerned not so much about the use of the native language but about the delaying the use of English" (p. 275). Thus, early instruction in both languages can promote both goals and can be used as the foundation of a two-way bilingual program that promotes Spanish acquisition for English-only children.

Lily Wong Fillmore (1976, 1979, 1991, 2000) has also documented the loss of language and cultural patterns among U.S. immigrant populations. She describes the pain and personal sense of loss that she experienced as a Chinese immigrant when she lost the ability to communicate with family members and the sense of shame associated with their family cultural practices. Wong Fillmore concludes the following:

> *An early English-only focus is not necessarily better here. It is true that children in the preschool years can learn a language quickly and with little apparent effort. These are the years of rapid language development and children can acquire a language in a year or two simply by being in a setting where the language is in daily use. However, it is equally true that languages can be lost with equal ease during this period, especially when the language they are learning is more highly valued than the language they already speak. Over the years, I have tracked many young children who, as soon as they learn a little English in the school, put aside the language they already know and speak, and choose to communicate exclusively in English, even at home with family members who do not speak or understand much English. (Wong Fillmore, 2000, p. 37)*

A recent large study examined the impact of bilingualism and school instructional variables on language and literacy outcomes in students (K-5) in Miami-Dade

County, Florida (Oller & Eilers, 2002). They included for analysis the SES of the family, the language spoken at home, as well as the instructional methods of the school. Children were assessed in both Spanish and English on an array of standardized and more open-ended language and reading measures. For monolingual English-speaking children instructed in only English, "differences favoring monolinguals were relatively large at kindergarten and 2nd grade, but notably smaller or absent by 5th grade, suggesting that bilingual children's abilities were improving relative to monolingual peers across the elementary years" (p. 282). For Spanish-speaking children learning English, they concluded, "Thus, it seems inevitable to conclude that Two-way education as opposed to English Immersion showed few if any long-term advantages or disadvantages with regard to language and literacy in English, but that Two-way education showed significant advantages for bilingual children in acquisition of language and literacy in Spanish" (p. 285). An unexpected finding of their research was that "Spanish appears to be losing ground rapidly in the Hispanic communities of Miami. . . . Data based on observations of usage of language in classrooms and hallways indicated a strong preference among Hispanic children for speaking English when given the choice, regardless of age or language background at home" (p. 291).

Two findings from this research are important for early childhood educators:

1. Education in both the home language and English did not delay English achievement and provided the added benefit of Spanish language literacy.
2. Spanish-speaking children in Miami from all backgrounds start to prefer to speak English very quickly.

Research on preschool-aged ELL children has shown that they can successfully learn two languages and experience multiple cognitive benefits when English acquisition is not at the expense of continued home language development (Bialystok, 2001; Espinosa & Burns, 2003; Winsler, Diaz, Espinosa, & Rodriguez, 1999; Rodriguez, Duran, Diaz, & Espinosa, 1995). In these studies, children who were systematically exposed to two languages during the preschool years demonstrated age-appropriate development in both languages as well as specific cognitive benefits associated with bilingualism.

In addition to supporting a child's home language, early childhood classrooms can intentionally promote the acquisition of English. However, when introducing children to English in an early childhood program, it is important to implement an *additive* model of English acquisition (where English and the home language are both supported) and not a subtractive model, where English is substituted for the home language (Garcia, 2003). When teachers and other school personnel communicate a respect and appreciation for the child's home language, and the family continues to use the first language, the child will value and show positive outcomes in both languages.

Other researchers (Thomas & Collier, 2002; August & Shanahan, 2006) studying this issue have also concluded that teaching reading skills to ELL children in the home language is more effective in the long run when measuring English language achievement outcomes; *immersing young children in English (even though they appear to pick it up quickly) does not lead to higher achievement in English in the long run.*

The important point to keep in mind for young ELL children is that their home language and cultural practices are fragile and susceptible to dominance by the English language and mainstream culture. Children who have the opportunity to speak two languages should be encouraged to maintain both, so they can enjoy the linguistic and cultural benefits that accompany bilingual status and cultivate their home language as well as English. Maintaining the home language is essential not just to the child's future academic and cognitive development, but also to the child's ability to establish a strong cultural identity, to develop and sustain strong ties with their immediate and extended families, and to thrive in a global, multilingual world (Garcia, 2003; Wong-Fillmore, 2000). In Chapter 6, I will describe methods that all teachers, even monolingual English-speaking teachers, can implement to actively encourage and support both continued home language development and English acquisition.

Question: Why do you think the continued use of the home language has such a strong influence on ELLs overall development?

BILINGUALISM AND SOCIAL-EMOTIONAL DEVELOPMENT

Because many young ELL children speak a language other than English in the home and enter early group care and/or educational settings that use English as the language of instruction, it is important to know how the development of bilingualism or the acquisition of English and the potential loss of home language affect the child's social competence. Developmental theory suggests that individual development is embedded within and shaped by social interaction and that knowledge is created by the interactions between teachers and students (National Scientific Council on the Developing Child, 2007a; Shonkhoff & Phillips, 2000). The concepts, perspectives, and cognitive constructs an individual develops are produced by shared social activities, values, and discussions. By studying the cultural and linguistic characteristics of the children, teachers, and peers, we can better understand the relationships among language, culture, social, and cognitive development (Garcia, 2005).

A young child's development of language proficiency is highly dependent on the cultural context of his early learning environment. The earliest interactions between children and significant others around them communicate to the child what types of language are valued, when one should talk, and how to use language as a tool for thinking. As children have learned these language skills in the highly specific cultural context of their homes, they must learn new communicative strategies in school settings. When linguistically diverse children enter school, they encounter classroom cultures that differ markedly from their familiar home culture. Children who are not native English speakers face many challenges because the language they have used to form their mental concepts and gain control over their cognitive processes is no longer dominant. The social and cognitive skills that have been developed through the use of one language and cultural context may no longer apply to this new setting. This linguistic and cultural disconnect, from a sociocultural perspective, would then place the child at risk for interrupted cognitive development and poor academic achievement (Diaz & Klinger, 1991).

For young children, language development and learning about one's own culture are closely linked.

> *Culture and linguistic identity provide a strong and important sense of self and family belonging, which in turn supports a wide range of learning capabilities, not the least of which is learning a second language. (Garcia, 1991, p. 2)*

There is considerable variation among families in the ways in which they socialize their young children into language and literacy use. It is important to remember that young children have formed culturally shaped expectations and attitudes for *when* they are supposed to talk, *whom* they should talk to, and *what type of language* is appropriate in different contexts. When the cultural expectations of the home and school vary markedly, the child may initially feel some discomfort and anxiety in the school setting. When a young child is taught to be silent in the company of adults and that it is disrespectful to draw attention to oneself, it is difficult for that child to enthusiastically raise his or her hand and make contributions to group discussions when that is the expectation of the school.(See example in box below.) Although most researchers agree that children can learn to successfully navigate two different cultures, educators need to be aware of the values and practices of the child's home environment to design classroom practices that support the child's successful transition.

There is much research that underscores the critical nature of children's social and emotional development to their long-term school and life success (Shonkoff & Philips, 2000; Ravler & Zigler, 1997; Wentzel & Asher, 1995). This research points to children's ability to positively build relationships with peers and adults as critical to their academic success. Specifically, current research suggests that preschool

---

Navigating Cultural Differences

In a program I supervised, teachers referred a 5-year-old to me, Maria, because she was not talking during group time and rarely volunteered information to the teachers. The teachers were concerned that this young ELL child who was getting ready to enter kindergarten was not assertive enough. She let other children speak for her and had never been observed raising her hand, even when she had something to say. Maria was observed talking and laughing with small groups of other ELL girls—but never in large groups or with the teachers. The teachers wanted me to design a plan with the parents that focused on helping her speak her mind and express herself more frequently.

When I met with the parents to discuss this concern, I could tell that they did not view Maria's behavior as a problem. They stated that they were raising Maria to be respectful, not aggressive. They wanted Maria to be obedient and not challenging. To them, having a child who talked a lot in class and asserted herself with her peers and teachers was not suitable. The suggestion that we might encourage Maria to speak her mind contradicted what the parents' believed was in Maria's best interests.

Question

How might I have reconciled these differing views of desirable behaviors while respecting the parents' cultural beliefs and supporting the teachers' goals for Maria?

children who learn to regulate their emotions in socially appropriate ways and control negative emotions do better in school (McClelland, Morrison, & Holmes, 2000). If young children can pay attention, follow directions, and get along with others, they are more likely to be perceived positively by their peers and teachers and become successful academically. When teachers view children's behavior positively, especially children at risk for poor outcomes, they are more likely to give them opportunities to participate and perceive them as having academic ability (Espinosa & Laffey, 2003; Rist, 1970, 2000).

Young children in the process of acquiring English as a second language face additional social-emotional challenges in the preschool setting. *Affective filter* is the term Stephen Krashen (1985) has used to refer to the cluster of negative emotional and motivational factors that may interfere with a child's ability to learn a second language efficiently. Such factors include anxiety, self-consciousness, embarrassment, and fear. According to Krashen, when a child's affective filter is aroused, the child will "shut down" and not actively engage in the process of learning English. Krashen claims that learners with high motivation, self-confidence, a good

It is important to attend to children's social and emotional development as they are learning a second language.

self-image, and a low level of anxiety are better equipped for success in second-language acquisition. Low motivation, low self-esteem, and debilitating anxiety can combine to "raise" the affective filter and form a "mental block" that interferes with the child's ability to process enriched language-learning opportunities. In other words, when the filter is "up" it impedes language acquisition. On the other hand, positive affect is necessary, but not sufficient on its own, for acquisition to take place (Krashen, 1985).

Researchers have found a consistent relation between various forms of anxiety and language learning in all situations, formal and informal, with school-age children. This is an important point when considering the role of social-emotional development for young ELL children because their emotional state as well as their social skills can influence their ability to successfully engage with English ELL opportunities so necessary for English acquisition and ultimate school success.

Clearly, the emotional and social health of young ELL children is important to their school adjustment and academic achievement. According to multiple measures of family risk factors (i.e., poverty, immigrant status, English language fluency, access to mental and physical health services), Latino ELL children would appear to be at greater risk for social-emotional difficulties than their White and non-Hispanic peers. However, when Robert Crosnoe (2004) analyzed kindergarten teachers' ratings of Mexican immigrant children's level of *internalizing symptoms* (e.g., anxiety, sadness) and *externalizing symptoms* (e.g., anger, fighting), he found that children from Mexican immigrant families had lower levels of internalizing and externalizing symptoms than both their White and African American peers. Crosnoe carefully separated out the teacher ratings for children from recent Mexican immigrant families to examine their perceived social-emotional competencies. The families had low levels of household income and education and low levels of English ability. In essence, despite family characteristics that typically are associated with delayed development, the teachers rated the children of Mexican immigrant families at kindergarten entry as more socially and emotionally competent than their peers from similar backgrounds.

It is possible that the Hispanic cultural emphasis on family cohesiveness, respect, and moral development that Mexican immigrant families bring with them to the United States may provide a foundation of social security for young Latinos—it may be part of their "funds of knowledge." Although Mexican immigrant families were characterized by low SES, high degrees of poverty, and lack of medical insurance, they also were more likely to have a two-parent family structure (Manning, 2005). These family cultural values and parenting customs could create a safe and secure early care environment for children from Mexican immigrant families. Serving the Hispanic community well for centuries, these family strengths need to be recognized and celebrated by early childhood programs.

This observed social-emotional strength of young Latinos may be a potential source of resilience that school personnel should recognize, support, and enhance. Because young Mexican immigrant children are judged to be at least as if not more intra- and interpersonally competent than their peers, something about Hispanic child-rearing practices has promoted their children's ability to control their emotions and get along with others at school entry—two highly prized social competencies for school success (Boyd et al., 2005). Low-income Hispanic parents clearly have the capacity to support their children's emotional security and social competence. The ways they support their children's development may not reflect traditional school practices, but nonetheless need to be respected, honored, and incorporated into the school culture (Lopez, 2001). In fact, Hispanic parents' commitment to their children and methods of early child rearing may represent a "great untapped resource" that could be better utilized within the school setting (Espinosa, 1995).

For young children who are ELLs, the relationship between their social-emotional development and personality characteristics and English acquisition is reciprocal: Their individual social competencies and personality traits influence their progress in English acquisition and the instructional methods used to teach them English influence their long-term social and cognitive development.

RESEARCH ON DIFFERENT CURRICULUM AND PROGRAM APPROACHES

In English-only programs (sometimes called *submersion programs*), ELL students are expected to learn English from the beginning and any support for the child's home language is intended to merely help the child cope with an all-English classroom. In these classrooms, English is used almost exclusively and most print is in English. The child may have some English as a second language (ESL) instruction— usually in a pull-out format—to promote rapid acquisition of enough English to comprehend English instruction. In some English preschool classrooms, ELL children are offered home language support by support staff or through translations, multilingual materials, and active family involvement practices. However, the primary goal of these programs is the rapid acquisition of English and the attainment of learning expectations in English. In practice, there is much variability in how much support and attention is paid to the home language in English-dominant preschool programs (Chang et al., 2007).

Bilingual programs can be described in multiple ways: transitional, maintenance of home language, one-way or two-way, and dual language bilingual programs. In all bilingual classrooms, instruction is divided between English and the child's home language. However, the goals in a transitional program focus on using the home language to "bridge" into English. On the other hand, in a two-way dual language program a portion of the students are native English speakers and all participants are expected to become bilingual and biliterate in a second language: for ELL students it is English and for English-speaking students it is usually Spanish. One-way developmental bilingual programs typically include only ELL students, although they share the goals of bilingualism and biliteracy for the ELL participants.

Bilingual programs also differ in the amount of classroom time spent using English and the non-English language for instructional purposes. The two most common approaches are 90:10 and 50:50. In 90:10 models, students receive 90% of their instruction in a language other than English (usually Spanish) and 10% of their instruction in English initially while gradually increasing the amount of English over several years. In 50:50 models, the classroom time is divided roughly equally between English and the non-English language throughout the duration of the program.

Bilingual education, how it is implemented, and whether it is effective continues to generate much controversy in the United States. What is clear from the conclusions of multiple studies and several syntheses of research is that an English-only or English submersion approach is not more effective than bilingual approaches. In fact, the Report of the National Literacy Panel on Language-Minority Children and Youth stated the following:

> *Research indicates that instructional programs work when they provide opportunities for students to develop proficiency in their first language. Studies that compare bilingual instruction with English-only instruction demonstrate that language-minority students instructed in their native-language as well as in English perform better, on average, on measures of English reading proficiency than language-minority students instructed only in English. (August & Shanahan, 2006, p. 5)*

Currently, it is difficult to determine with any precision the most common type of program model available for ELL children during the early childhood years. There are several published studies of carefully implemented dual language programs and a growing literature on English language preschool approaches for ELL children. However, when one reviews the state-level early childhood standards and the state- and national-level preschool program evaluations, it appears that most programs do not implement a systematic approach to English acquisition with careful attention to home language proficiency and development (Gormley et al., 2005; Chang et al., 2007; Rodriguez et al., 1995; Winsler et al., 1999).

The decision of which type of program to offer ELL children can be influenced by state regulations (e.g., Proposition 227 in California, which severely limits bilingual programs in K-12), understanding of dual language development, program capacity to support multiple languages, and parent–community values and priorities. However, this is a critical decision that requires staff, parent, and community consensus on language goals and methods to achieve those goals. The need for program goals will be discussed further in Chapter 6. See the following definition of dual language programs.

Dual Language Programs

Educational programs that intentionally use two languages can be one-way, two-way, 50:50, and/or 90:10 models.

- In one-way dual language programs, one language group is schooled in two languages. For example, native Spanish speakers are educated in Spanish and English.
- In two-way dual language programs, native English speakers and Spanish speakers are all schooled in English and Spanish, thereby resulting in dual language development for both groups. The percentage of instructional time in each language can be roughly equal amounts of time in each language, 50:50; or more focused time in the minority language, 90:10, with increasing amounts of time in English as the child progresses through the grades.

RESEARCH ON DUAL LANGUAGE APPROACHES In California, several studies of the impact of a bilingual program on children's home language in addition to their acquisition of English provided support for the positive influence of a dual language preschool on children's overall language and cognitive development (Rodriguez et al., 1995; Winsler et al., 1999). Children enrolled in the high-quality bilingual preschool program were compared to a matched monolingual Spanish-speaking comparison group. Rodriguez et al. and Winsler et al. both described the preschool program as being "truly bilingual," with equal amounts of instructional time spent in Spanish and English (roughly a 50-50 model), and "high quality," with a well-defined curriculum and ongoing assessment. Children enrolled in the bilingual preschool showed enhanced development in both Spanish and English acquisition over the comparison group. The ELL children in this study were from low-income Spanish-speaking families, most of who had recently immigrated to California from rural Mexico. The children in the dual language approach were advancing toward balanced bilingualism while gaining increasing mastery over the linguistic structures of both English and Spanish. They were also learning the academic skills identified as important to school readiness. These studies demonstrated that preschool-aged children, when provided an enriched dual language program, can make significant gains in English language fluency while also maintaining native language growth that exceeded their monolingual peers. The acquisition of English during the preschool years does not have to be at the expense of the home language if teachers carefully and systematically support both languages within the context of a high-quality preschool curriculum.

A more recent experimental study from New Jersey (Barnett, Yarosz, Thomas, Jung, & Blanco, 2007) also found a dual language program for preschool children when compared to English immersion "supported stronger Spanish language gains at no expense to English language development in both native English and native Spanish speakers" (Barnett et al., 2007, p. 20). This study tested preschoolers' language, literacy, and mathematical skills in the fall and again in the spring, testing the ELL children in both Spanish and English. Those children in the dual language program received all instruction in Spanish one week, then all instruction in English the next week, resulting in a 50:50 model. However, there was some support for Spanish in the English immersion program, depending on staff ability and child needs. All the ELL children in the dual language program made greater gains in their Spanish vocabulary while their peers in the English immersion program lost ground in their native language. This study concluded that ELL preschool children in a two-way immersion program can maintain and continue to develop their home language as they also acquired English at the same rate as those in an English-only program.

A recent meta-analysis of hundreds of studies from the National Literacy Panel on Language Minority Children and Youth, *Developing Literacy in Second Language Learners* (August & Shanahan, 2006), concluded that "English language learners may learn to read best if taught both in their native language and English from early in the process of formal schooling. Rather than confusing children, as some have feared, reading instruction in a familiar language may serve as a bridge to success in English because decoding, sound blending, and generic comprehension strategies clearly transfer between languages that use phonetic orthographies, such as Spanish, French, and English" (August, 2002; August & Hakuta, 1997; Fitzgerald, 1995a, 1995b; Garcia, 2000) (p. 397). Although the panel cautioned the readers that the findings do not identify potentially moderating variables that most likely are influential in making bilingual instruction maximally effective for all students (such as quality of instruction), their findings consistently favored dual language or bilingual instructional approaches for ELL children.

In addition, other recent large-scale studies have also found that those ELL students who receive at least 50% of their instruction in their native language for at least four years are the most likely of all ELL students to fully reach the 50th percentile on nationally normed achievement tests in both their home language and English in all subjects. They are also the least likely to drop out of high school (Thomas & Collier, 2002).

A recent policy report by Eugene Garcia and Bryant Jensen (2007) has also advocated for dual language approaches based on the empirical evidence. They describe the rationale for dual language programs, review multiple studies focusing on literacy and writing outcomes, and conclude that "dual language immersion is an excellent model for academic achievement for all children. It has been shown to promote English language learning as well or better than other special programs designed for language minority children. . . . Dual language immersion programs also appear to encourage achievement in academic subjects in both English and the minority languages" (p. 4). Their final conclusion seems to sum up the consensus of most researchers in this area: "Having all U.S. students become fluent in more than one language is not only a marketable skill in today's increasingly diverse and global society, but, as the studies mentioned demonstrate, it can also contribute to increased cognitive flexibility and high achievement in math, science and language arts" (p. 6).

TRANSFER OF EARLY LITERACY SKILLS FROM SPANISH TO ENGLISH   One of the ongoing debates in the education of ELL children is which language to use during early literacy instruction. Some scholars in this area have suggested that young children will be confused and their acquisition of English fluency and literacy skills will be delayed if they are not instructed in English-only programs from the very beginning. Others have argued that skills in the first language will aid in developing skills in the second language (Cummins, 1994). The National Literacy Panel on Language–Minority Children and Youth concluded that the available evidence supports the transfer of knowledge from the first language to the second in certain domains: word reading (if both languages have similar orthographies), spelling, vocabulary with the use of cognates, reading comprehension, reading strategies, and certain aspects of writing. Most studies on this topic that focus specifically on the transfer of phonological processing skills between Spanish and English among young children also supported cross-language transfer (Oller & Eilers, 2002; Leafsted & Gerber, 2005).

Recent research on the transfer of preschool literacy skills from Spanish to English has supported the transfer hypothesis as well. Lisa Lopez and her colleagues at Harvard and the University of Miami have conducted a series of studies on Hispanic Head Start children. They found that "oral language skills in Spanish influence phonological awareness in English" (Lopez & Greenfield, 2004, p. 12).

Based on their research on Head Start children in the Miami-Dade County Head Start programs, they argued, "Building on a child's language abilities in his or her L1 [native/home language] will not only help the child fully master that language, but provide him or her with the tools to deconstruct the L2 [new language]. Early development of language skills, such as semantics, syntax, narrative discourse, and morphology, as well as phonological awareness, will provide the child with a "meta" understanding of language that he or she can apply to language development and literacy skills in the L2" (p. 13).

The conclusions from these studies suggest the following:

- Young children are quite capable of learning academic content in two languages.
- Children may benefit cognitively from learning more than one language.
- Transitioning to English too soon may cost children in the long run.
- Many early language and literacy skills learned in Spanish clearly transfer to English.

The children who were taught in English-only classrooms or transitioned to English instruction before they demonstrated well-established oral language abilities in their own language and had achieved high levels of English oral fluency did not fare as well as those who had the opportunity to learn through two languages (Espinosa, 2008b).

HOW MUCH INSTRUCTION IN THE HOME LANGUAGE?   Although there is a small but growing body of research on the impact of dual language versus English-immersion approaches during the early years, there are very few empirical studies that can offer guidance on *how much* native language should be spoken, represented, and emphasized in the preschool classroom when the primary goal is to promote English fluency and English literacy. Teachers must grapple with the daily challenges of which language to use during which parts of the day, and how long the home language should be supported when the children appear to becoming fluent in English. Many programs also lack the personnel and/or the resources to fully implement dual language approaches.

A recent study by researchers at University of North Carolina and the Frank Porter Graham Child Development Institute (Chang et al., 2007) sheds some light on the question of the impact of English-only versus some support for the child's home language (Spanish). This study examined the relationship between language interactions and Spanish-speaking prekindergarten children's social and language development. The children studied and the data examined were from two large-scale studies of state-funded prekindergarten programs across 11 states and included more than 700 schools/centers and 345 Spanish-speaking children. The researchers recorded the quantity and quality of language interactions as well as the language in which the interaction occurred. Over the course of one prekindergarten school year, the Spanish-dominant children received less than 20% (17.3%) of their total language interactions with teachers in Spanish; in addition, only about one quarter (23%) of the children received any interactions at all in Spanish. The teachers in these classrooms used English two-thirds of the time when they were addressing a Spanish-speaking child; however, Spanish-speaking teachers had significantly more interactions with Spanish-speaking children and they tended to have more elaborated conversations (Chang et al., 2007).

The amount of Spanish spoken was significantly related to teachers' ratings of children's social competence: The more that children experienced English, the higher they were rated on having conduct and learning problems and the lower they were rated on frustration tolerance. Teachers' perceptions of their relationships with Spanish-speaking children also varied according to the language used in interactions. Spanish-speaking teachers not only spoke more frequently to Spanish-speaking children, they also rated their relationships with these children as closer than teachers who spoke less Spanish. Those teachers who spoke the least amount of Spanish rated their relationships with Spanish-speaking children as having more conflict and the children as having more problem behaviors. Neither the amount of Spanish spoken nor the amount of English spoken was related to children's English proficiency. The authors conclude that an English-only approach in early childhood programs is not in the best interests of ELLs and may fuel the achievement gap between different racial, ethnic, and socioeconomic groups rather than reduce the gap.

Although this study does not explicitly address the question of how much home language needs to be spoken to ELL children, it clearly reveals that using only English in prekindergarten classrooms with ELL children affects their opportunities to have rich language interactions and close relationships with their teachers. Other researchers (Pearson, 2001) have found that in order for young children to develop fluency in any language, they need to use it at least 25% of the time. If we combine the results of the research available, it is plausible to infer that young ELL children need at least 25% of their language interactions and instruction in English to develop English proficiency and at least 25% in their home language to develop academic mastery in both languages. It is difficult to specify with any accuracy how much of the remaining time should be devoted to which language. However, there is well-designed research that documents the positive benefits for young ELL children when they participate in 50:50 dual language programs that are based on high-quality, enriched curricula.

Additive versus Subtractive Bilingualism

Many researchers and experts in dual-language development make a distinction between *additive* bilingualism, in which the first language continues to be developed and the first culture is valued while the second language (usually English) is added; and *subtractive* bilingualism, in which the second language is added at the expense of the first language and culture, which diminish as a consequence (Cummins, 1994).

We now know some important aspects of young ELLs' development as well as features of learning environments that promote long-term growth and school achievement. Many ELL children are from low-income households where their parents have low levels of formal education. However, this finding is closely related to the language spoken in the home and the circumstances surrounding the family's immigration to the United States. In general, the current research base is revealing similar conclusions:

- Educators need to attend to the social-emotional development of ELL children as well as their cognitive development.
- Program approaches must provide some level of support for the home language.

- Young ELL children can learn English during the preschool years, but it must be an *additive* approach where English is added to the home language and not a *subtractive* approach where English is learned at the expense of an ELL child's home language.
- Specific instructional approaches must be adapted to the unique needs of children not fully proficient in English.

WORKING WITH FAMILIES OF CHILDREN WHO ARE ELLs

The importance of families, and particularly parents, in the growth and development of all children has been well documented for decades (Landry & Smith, 2005; Neuman & Celano, 2001; Snow et al., 1998). Establishing strong relationships with parents and extended family members is a major objective of most early childhood programs. Much research supports the idea that early childhood teachers need to understand, respect, and build upon families' cultural habits, beliefs, and behaviors (August & Shanahan, 2006; Barone & Xu, 2008; Nissani, 1990; Tabors, 1997/2008).

The data-based research on working with parents and families of ELL children has revealed that these parents have the desire and often the ability to help their children succeed academically (August & Shanahan, 2006; Brooker, 2002; Goldenberg, 1987). This line of research has shown that frequently schools misinterpret parents' behaviors and do not take advantage of ELL parents' potential contributions (Espinosa, 1995, 1998). As discussed in Chapter 2, families from different cultural groups may engage in practices that support language and literacy, but do so in culturally specific ways. For example, Latino parents may emphasize oral traditions of storytelling with moral themes and less on early storybook reading (Lopez et al., 2006). Latino parents may also believe they are responsible for teaching moral values while teachers are the experts on academic matters, so they show respect by not interfering with school practices. Teachers may misunderstand some of these parental behaviors; they could easily conclude that Latino parents are not engaged and committed to their children's school success when they do not attend school functions. The research suggests otherwise—which is why it is important for early childhood educators to be familiar with current scientific evidence.

Many barriers have been identified that make it difficult for ELL parents to actively engage with school programs. Two scholars from Arizona State University found five types of barriers that interfere with ELL parents' school involvement:

1. school-based barriers, primarily the view on the part of school officials that ELL parents, in various ways, lack the ability to become involved;
2. parents' lack of English language proficiency;
3. parental educational level;
4. mismatches between school culture and home culture; and
5. logistical issues, such as work hours and transportation limitations that make it difficult for ELL parents to attend school conferences (Arias & Morillo-Campbell, 2008).

When ELL parents do not respond to traditional methods of school involvement opportunities, such as PTA meetings or parent conferences, staff may view

ELL parents as "the problem" rather than adapting their expectations and approaches (Lopez, 2001). ELL parents have reported experiencing confusion and frustration with school systems that misunderstand their cultural beliefs and values, offering only rigid approaches to parental involvement (Arias & Morillo-Campbell, 2008; Lopez, 2001). Some ELL parents also find it uncomfortable to attend school functions when no one there speaks their language and they may not feel welcome.

Parent involvement programs that have shown positive results for ELL families and children have generally shared these characteristics:

1. employed practices that are culturally and linguistically appropriate for their families (e.g., they provide all communications in the families' preferred language and have bilingual and bicultural staff on site);

2. provided comprehensive services (e.g., they focus their curriculum on each child's total needs, not just on a narrow band of cognitive skills, and they make home visits and help parents meet a range of needs) (Delgado-Gaitan, 2001);

3. promoted high levels of reciprocal communication [they engaged in two-way communication that enlisted parents as partners and not just recipients of school information (Epstein, 2001)]; and

4. mobilized parents to advocate for the educational needs of their children.

What is clear from the current research is that ELL parents care deeply about their children's academic success, often have untapped skills and talents, and can make important contributions to their children's schooling. It is also clear that schools may need to adapt their methods of working with ELL parents. Early childhood educators can increase the chances of academic success for ELL children if the school environment fosters school–home collaboration through nontraditional

Teachers and parents of young children who are ELL gain important insights from each other when they work together.

methods. The school programs that effectively engaged ELL parents integrated the family into the school culture and employed the following methods:

1. Develop a reciprocal understanding of schools and families; they did not use a unidirectional model of communication.
2. Situate cultural strengths of family and community within the school community.
3. Provide parental education that includes family literacy and understanding school community.
4. Promote parental advocacy that informs and teaches parents how to advocate for their children.
5. Instill parental empowerment through parent-initiated efforts at the school and community level.
6. Implement culturally and linguistically appropriate practices in all aspects of communication (Arias & Morillo-Campbell, 2008).

Early childhood programs can establish effective relationships with ELL parents, but they will need to expand their methods to include, honor, and respect the cultural and linguistic strengths that families possess.

Summary

There is a growing research base that challenges common beliefs about the development of young ELLs. We now know some important aspects of young ELLs' development and have a much clearer picture of how two languages influence a child's overall growth. We also are identifying the features of learning environments that promote long-term growth and school achievement. The contribution of the child's home language to English language proficiency and school achievement is also better understood—although we still have a lot to learn about the cognitive processes involved when a young child learns basic concepts through two languages.

Many ELL children are from low-income households where their parents have low levels of formal education. However, this finding is closely related to the language spoken in the home and the circumstances surrounding the family's immigration to the United States. As stated previously, the current research base is revealing similar conclusions: educators need to attend to the social-emotional development of ELL children as well as their cognitive and literacy development; program approaches must provide some level of support for the home language; young ELL children can successfully learn English during the preschool years, but it must be an *additive* approach in which English is added to the home language and not a *subtractive* approach in which English is learned at the expense of the child's home language; and specific instructional approaches must be adapted to the unique needs of children who are not fully proficient in English.

The research base for establishing positive working relationships with ELL families is not as deep or robust as the research on working with native English-speaking families, but it nevertheless affirms the importance of these relationships and suggests that effective programs will need to design new methods. Programs will need to make adjustments for the language abilities and preferences of families as well as their cultural practices and beliefs. To make these adjustments, early childhood staff will need to learn about each family's language use and preferences, their cultural values and customs, as well as their aspirations for their children.

Reflection and Discussion Questions

1. Have you ever met an adult whose first language was not English? To what extent is he or she still fluent in the first language? What were the circumstances around this person's earliest exposure to English? Does this adult have any feelings about how the home language was or was not maintained?

2. Have you ever visited a classroom where some of the children were not native English speakers? What did you observe about their behavior? How did they interact with their peers and teachers?

3. Have you ever tried to teach a child who did not understand English? Describe your experiences.

4. Why do you think the home language has such a strong influence on ELL children's overall development?

5. What challenges have you observed in establishing close working relationships with families who do not speak English? Have any approaches been particularly successful for you?

Promising Curriculum, Instructional, and Assessment Strategies for Young English Language Learners

The research base shows that attending to the social, emotional and cognitive skills of dual language learners in early childhood enhances their schooling experiences. Children from linguistic minority households also require language instruction which is sensitive to their unique backgrounds. Instruction in oral language proficiency, vocabulary, and preliteracy skills provides a strong foundation for later success. In particular, it is crucial that educators understand how best to effectively support the home language so that early literacy can be fostered in the home as well as school.

BALLANTYNE, SANDEERMAN, D'EMILIO, & McLAUGHLIN, 2008, P. 35

The early childhood profession urgently needs guidance on how to apply the research evidence and scientific findings I have just discussed to our curriculum and assessment practices. We need to refine our thinking about "best practices" for young children who do not speak English as their first language. In addition, we need to know how to assess ELLs' developmental and academic progress and how to build competencies during the early childhood years that will promote long-term school and life success. These strategies are discussed in this chapter.

IMPORTANCE OF GOALS

I have found that one of the most important steps for any early childhood program is to collectively decide on explicit language goals for their ELLs. This process of developing a shared vision and programwide consensus on the desired outcomes serves as a useful reference point when making decisions about specific strategies. Without such clearly stated and explicit goals, many programs migrate toward practices that promote rapid English acquisition at the expense of the child's home language, or sometimes resort to a haphazard approach with no clear direction. Much recent research has found that the home language and cultural practices of young ELL children are fragile and susceptible to dominance by the English language and mainstream culture (Genesee et al., 2004).

Many well-intentioned early childhood teachers and administrators have implicit beliefs about the value of immersing the child in English versus maintaining the child's home language as the road to academic success. (See Myths About ELLs in Chapter 5.) These deeply held beliefs about the role of home language and the early acquisition of English can unconsciously influence the classroom teacher's use of language and send messages to the children about which language is more highly valued.

One large citywide preschool program that I worked with over two years had an enrollment of over 90% Spanish-speaking children from low-income homes. The staff professed a desire to support the children's home language and incorporated many multicultural activities, Spanish language books, and culturally appropriate materials. However, during the second year, when I videotaped their daily lessons and activities, I found that 80% to 90% of their instructional and language interactions were in English. The most striking finding from the videotapes was that the staff, all of who were fluent in Spanish and English, spoke almost exclusively in English during the instructional time (small group, large group, and individual tutoring), using Spanish for transitions, group management, and simple directions. For example, the teacher might say to the child, *"Venga aqui"* (come here) and then commence to instruct the child in English, i.e., "We are going to write in your journal now. What did you see at the zoo yesterday?" Although this emphasis on English language instruction might help foster English achievement, it is also sending messages about the value of each language that may eventually contribute to home language loss.

A program that has qualified bilingual staff and bilingual resources might decide to implement a dual language program and agree to the following language goal:

> *All children in ABC program will learn two languages. The native English speakers will learn Spanish (or Japanese, Chinese, Vietnamese, and so on) and the non-native English speakers will learn English. Our goal*

is for all children to eventually become bilingual and biliterate and to function competently in a multicultural setting.

In contrast, a program whose children speak many different languages and has few if any qualified bilingual educators might decide on the following goal for the ELL children enrolled:

The language of instruction in XYZ Preschool shall be primarily English. In addition, XYZ Preschool believes in the value of supporting the ongoing development of each ELL child's home language and family culture. Instructional activities, classroom materials, family interactions, and all communications shall respect, value, and incorporate the home language and culture to the maximum extent possible.

Once all staff have thoroughly discussed the language goals for ELL children, then specific instructional methods and materials, curriculum approaches, and assessment procedures can be designed. This explicit statement of language goals for non-native English speakers will turn out to be critical as the program decides on the primary language of instruction, the methods to support each child's home language, how to assess progress, and outreach approaches to families who may speak a different language and hold distinct cultural values. I have found that educators' beliefs matter. In fact, your deeply held beliefs and attitudes toward language development, and whether you believe that being exposed to more than one language will confuse a preschool child and delay English acquisition or contribute to overall cognitive growth and English fluency, will influence how you respond to each child's attempts to communicate, coloring your daily interactions.

Unless you believe "in your bones" that having a second language in addition to English is a gift and not a disadvantage, and that diversity is a resource not a problem to be solved, you are likely to respond to ELL children in ways that discourage the continued use of their home language—especially if you are not fluent in the child's home language.

SPECIFIC TEACHING STRATEGIES IN DUAL LANGUAGE EARLY CHILDHOOD PROGRAMS

Many policy reports and program evaluations recommend that early childhood programs provide support for ongoing development of each child's home language. Most often, very few specific practices are included in these recommendations. Therefore, programs are often left with little clear-cut guidance on *how* to design and implement practices that promote both English acquisition and the development of the home language. The following is a discussion of how to implement a dual language approach.

WHAT DOES A HIGH-QUALITY DUAL LANGUAGE PROGRAM LOOK LIKE?   As each program develops specific language and/or literacy goals for its ELL children and native English speakers, it will be important to also make explicit the amount of instructional time that will be devoted to which language. If your program decides on a 50:50 dual language program, you can implement this model in a variety of ways.

Some of the research described in Chapter 5 implemented an A.M.-P.M. (or morning and afternoon) approach to language of instruction; they spoke English in the A.M. and Spanish in the P.M. (Rodriguez et al., 1995; Winsler et al., 1999). In this case, the staffing patterns and language fluency of the staff required this configuration. During the English portion of the day, English was the primary language used during instruction, transitions, and individual interactions. At this time, Spanish was used only when children clearly did not understand what was expected and a Spanish-speaking adult was available. The same principles were applied during the Spanish-only portion of the day. The program was careful to implement similar curriculum content during each session and alternated the A.M.-P.M. language times each week.

Other dual language program models (included in the research described earlier) have implemented language models that alternate the language of instruction each week—and have the children move from the Spanish language room with its Spanish-speaking staff to the English language room with its English-speaking staff weekly (Barnett et al., 2006). The common characteristic is the intentional and systematic shifting between each language so that it works out to be approximately 50:50 with comparable academic content taught in both languages. This approach can work for all language groups, both English language learners and native English speakers.

WHO TEACHES IN WHICH LANGUAGE?   When implementing a dual language approach, it is ideal to have staff at all levels, from paraprofessionals to resource specialists, who are fully fluent in English and the children's home language. Often this is not possible when communities are undergoing rapid demographic shifts and many new cultures and languages are represented. However, even when it is difficult to reflect all languages spoken by children and families, programs need to actively recruit fully qualified teachers who are skilled in all aspects of early childhood curricula and fluent in multiple languages. The tendency to employ teacher aides and parent volunteers who represent the languages and cultures of the families is an important part of the staffing process—but not nearly enough. When instructional activities with academic content can only be led by monolingual English speakers, it sends a message to the children and families that English is the high-value language and their home language is mainly used for secondary activities. This is a major challenge for the early childhood profession, but it cannot be ignored and must be aggressively addressed.

The other side of this issue also needs to be discussed. As I travel around the country working with early childhood professionals, they often want to know about their staff (often recently hired) who are native speakers of the child's home language but not fully fluent in English. They describe well-intentioned paraprofessionals who are able to provide comfort and guidance in the child's home language, but not much assistance in English—that, or they speak broken, ungrammatical English. Although I fully support the intentional hiring of a more diverse workforce (indeed, it is a professional imperative), I also know that all children need to have competent language models who can communicate with them using standard language representations. To have complex, extended conversations in a linguistically rich classroom environment, all staff need to commit to improving both their pedagogy skills as well as their ability to use multiple languages fluently and correctly. This may require ongoing professional development

Early childhood teachers can discuss picture books with ELL children in their home language in addition to English.

for both native English-speaking staff and those who speak the child's home language but who are not fully fluent in English.

THE IMPORTANCE OF A COMPREHENSIVE CURRICULUM

The research repeatedly stresses the importance of a high-quality, comprehensive curriculum for all children—especially for ELL children. Programs that implement curricula that address all aspects of early development (and not just cognitive or early literacy skills) by highly qualified teachers consistently outperform more limited models. Comprehensive curricula are not focused solely on literacy skills or cognitive development; they attend to children's social-emotional and motor development, as well as their overall health. Comprehensive curricula also actively partner with parents and often provide extended services for families. A recent report from the National Center for Children in Poverty, *Effective Preschool Curricula and Teaching Strategies* (Klein & Knitzer, 2006), concludes that high-quality preschool programs can reduce the achievement gap for children from low-income homes, but they need to include the following:

- an intentional curriculum that is research based;
- teachers who are actively engaged with all young children;
- a focus on social and regulatory skills;
- adaptations to cultural and linguistic diversity;
- focused, direct, intentional instructional interactions;
- new ways of assessing student progress and classroom quality; and
- effective teacher professional development and support.

These features of high-quality curricula are just as important for English language learners as for native English speakers—but they are not enough. Good instruction for children in general tends to be good for ELLs in particular. However, in addition to clear, intentional interactions that are focused on important instructional goals, ELL children also require adaptations while they are in the process of acquiring English. The most recent research tells us that the achievement of ELL children is positively influenced by the same instructional variables as native English speakers, but to a lesser extent (August & Shanahan, 2006). These studies suggest that the elements of effective instruction in general ought to be the foundation of instruction for ELL students—*however, ELL students need curriculum enhancements or accommodations* (Goldenberg, 2006).

ELL students, like their native English-speaking peers, will benefit from the following teaching and learning strategies:

- active engagement,
- connections to their existing knowledge,
- opportunities to practice and apply new information,
- frequent reviews and practice,
- direct instruction on certain aspects of literacy,
- special attention to English vocabulary and English oral language development, and
- instructional accommodations to keep pace with their native English-speaking peers.

Claude Goldenberg (2006), a professor of education at Stanford University who has extensively researched bilingualism for young children, has recommended the following instructional supports for ELL students based on his review of three recent large national studies of bilingual students:

- strategic use of the primary language (e.g., when introducing concepts or new activities, be sure to use the child's home language before introducing the concept in English so each child will understand the concept),
- consistent expectations, instruction, and routines;
- extended explanations and opportunities for practice;
- use of physical gestures and visual cues;
- focusing on the similarities/differences (cognates) between English and Spanish (home language) (e.g., make a point to use objects with Spanish–English cognates like *telephone/teléfono*, show the object and point out the English word and the Spanish word—their similarities and differences);
- extra practice reading words, sentences, and stories;
- focus on vocabulary development and check frequently for children's comprehension (e.g., highlight key words in English while reading story books by explaining their meaning, offering synonyms, and using them in different contexts while frequently interacting with children to see if they understand the meaning of the words); and
- paraphrasing students' language and encouraging them to expand.

The amount and quality of research on preschool instructional approaches for ELL children is not extensive. Although the NELP had over 1700 studies of early literacy to review, of which more than 300 were rigorous, well-designed studies, the number of experimental studies examining the effectiveness of different curriculum models on preschool ELLs school achievement is at best in the dozens. In general, most of the findings from the NELP for native English speakers also apply to ELL children ages 3 to 6—however, again, curricular adaptations must be made. Reading books aloud to children is important for all children's later literacy (National Early Literacy Panel Report, 2008), but the procedures used may need to be adjusted for ELL children. For instance, the Nuestros Niños Early Language and Literacy Program (Castro, Gillanders, Buysse, & Machado-Casas, 2005), developed at the Frank Porter Graham Child Development Institute of the University of North Carolina, has suggested the following practices for Spanish-speaking preschoolers:

1. Engage the children in pre-reading activities that identify key words and phrases that are essential to understanding the text; help the ELL children learn the key vocabulary by translating into Spanish (or home language) and using multisensory materials to illustrate the book meaning. (For example, provide objects described or included in the story so that children can hold them and associate the object with the word. In the popular book *Caps for Sale*, teachers can hand out different hats and have the children try them on while emphasizing the words *hat, brown, head, on top of,* and so on.)
2. Use good book-reading strategies including dialogic reading practices (described in more detail below under specific book-reading strategies) that prompt the children to interact and respond to the story. While interacting with the children during reading, the teacher will also need to consider which stage of English acquisition the child is in and adapt expectations accordingly (the stages are described in more detail in Chapter 5).
3. After reading books to children, provide opportunities for using the core vocabulary from the book in conversations and related extension activities (Castro et al., p. 79).

In summary, the research on ELL achievement suggests that recommended instruction is similar to good instruction for English-speaking children. High-quality instruction for all students also benefits ELL students; however, they need instructional enhancements and attention to the social-emotional climate as they become fluent in two languages—their home language and English. The evidence also underscores the need to provide special attention to English vocabulary and English oral language development for ELL children. With support for the home language and accommodations for English acquisition, ELL children are able to achieve multiple linguistic and cultural competencies.

SPECIFIC STRATEGIES IN ENGLISH LANGUAGE PROGRAMS WITH HOME LANGUAGE SUPPORT

Once you have decided on the language goals of your program and have chosen a model of instruction that supports your goals (i.e., dual language, 50:50, or primarily English instruction with home language support, 90:10), then you must decide who will provide instruction in which language during which parts of the day. I often consult with programs that have little or no staff that speak the home language of the children. They will question whether they have the capacity to support the ongoing development of the children's native language when they cannot use it during instructional activities or everyday interactions. At this point, it is important to refer back to the language goals of the program as well as the individual language goals for each child.

Even when teachers and ancillary staff do not speak the child's home language, there are many specific teaching practices that will support native language development throughout the day in all kinds of learning situations. In addition, educators need to provide long-term help to build literacy skills in children's primary language. The resources and expertise to implement some or all of the necessary strategies can be found in the list that follows.

To focus only on the acquisition of English and to not explicitly prioritize the ongoing development of each child's home language will most likely lead to the fading of home language abilities over time. So, although introducing young ELL children to English while also supporting development of their home language even when you do not speak it and have no experience with the language can seem like a challenging, overwhelming goal, especially when many languages are represented in a single program, it is possible and should be a high-priority goal. In fact, even in programs with all English-speaking children, it is often desirable to introduce children to a second language.

The following specific practices have been shown through prior research to help young ELL children acquire English while also supporting the continued development of their home language:

1. Recruit bilingual paraprofessionals, assistants, family members, community volunteers, and/or older, more competent students to interact with, read to, and assist ELL children, individually or in small groups. Hearing their home language during valuable class time—especially hearing it read, will communicate the importance and status of the language of the home. In addition, those proficient in the child's home language can teach new words to the whole class, thus promoting a dual language approach. By giving the home language attention, status, and value, the chances are increased that ELL children will continue to speak it with family members and experience the advantages of knowing more than one language.

2. Incorporate the children's home language into the daily classroom activities through song, poetry, dances, rhymes, and counting. There are many authentic, multicultural literature books designed for young children that are written in two languages. Many will have English on one side of the page and the second language on the other side. A staff member fluent in English can read the English text and a staff member or volunteer fluent in the second language can read the second language text. A good example of this kind of book for English and Spanish speakers is *Pío Peep: Traditional Spanish Nursery Rhymes* (Ada & Campoy, 2004). Fortunately, there are many literature books, resource books, alphabet books, dictionaries, and songbooks written in two languages that are culturally and developmentally appropriate and are quite appealing to young children. Increasingly, there are also dual language

materials, animated stories, songs, and picture books available on the Internet, some of which are free! Appendix B contains a sampling of materials available in multiple languages.

3. Use children's personal histories to create *identity texts*. Judith Bernhard, professor of early childhood education and researcher of bilingual education, and her colleagues have designed and evaluated an early literacy intervention for preschool and primary ELL children, the Early Authors Program, which links the child's home culture with early reading and writing activities (Bernhard, Cummins, Campoy, Ada, Winsler, & Bleiker, 2006). The children collaborate with family members, friends, caregivers, and teachers to create "identity texts" in which the children themselves are the main characters. By talking about, writing about, reading about, and publicly sharing their personal life histories, children are able to develop pride in themselves, create a positive orientation to literacy, and create meaningful and engaging text. This approach has been shown to result in improved language scores and enhanced reading comprehension. Appendix C contains a detailed description of this approach with reference materials.

4. Use picture books and photo albums to make up stories with the children. These can be told in any language and encourage participation of all children. Parents and other family members can also use these books to engage in extended conversations about shared experiences, family customs, recent outings, and/or different kinds of animals. These shared book readings are also an excellent time to explicitly point out vocabulary in both languages.

5. Use small-group "read-alouds" with ELL children and native English speakers. You can choose from a variety of books, but be sure to read books that are interesting to young children, culturally appropriate, and related to both the children's background and the main theme of the week. Ideally, books used for read-alouds have rich and rare vocabulary that can be extended to cross-curricular activities. Predictable books are especially good for ELL children because they help children not fully fluent in English anticipate what will happen and participate in the reading. They also frequently use interesting rhyme and alliteration that promote phonological awareness. Appendix B contains a list of resources including suggested predictable books, big books, poetry books, rhyme books, and songbooks as well as informational books that are appropriate for young read-alouds with ELL children.

6. Having young children take pictures of their "world outside of school" has also been shown to increase conversation between ELL children and teachers (Penn State Newsletter, 2009). After the children take multiple pictures of important events outside of their school day, they can be asked to share their favorites with a teacher. This will promote more interaction between the ELL children and teachers, improve the teacher's understanding of the each ELL child's language abilities, and support English conversational skills for the ELLs. Having the children describe their own pictures is a great way to increase the amount of complex language interactions between teachers and young children who are in the early stages of learning English.

7. When reading with ELL children, it is important to allow them to use their home language as well as English during reading activities.

8. Review key concepts and vocabulary before reading the book. Encourage the children to predict what will happen in the story—in the language in which they are most fluent. Show pictures or concrete representations (i.e., flannel board pictures) of key vocabulary and *chunks of language*. With ELL children it is important to frequently check their understanding in English. You can do this by asking them direct questions, asking them to hold up flannel board figures, asking them to stand up during key parts of the story or to demonstrate in other ways that they understand the story narrative and vocabulary used.

9. Make connections between the content of the story and the children's own life experiences. During these discussions, be sure to allow enough time for the ELL children to formulate their thoughts and express themselves in their dominant language.

10. Keep the reading time short because ELL children may not have long attention spans as they are learning English—but gradually extend reading time as you see the children can maintain their attention. Strive to engage the children by using all your good book-reading strategies (e.g., let the children see the illustrations and print; use a dramatic reading voice to help the story "come alive"; use props, flannel boards, songs, rhymes, and concrete objects to promote understanding).

11. Use *dialogic reading techniques* (Whitehurst, 2004; see text box below) to encourage the children's active participation in the activity. By using prompts and systematically engaging in back-and-forth dialogue about the content of the book, teachers are helping children construct meaning and comprehend text.

12. During all reading activities, it is important for the teacher to know which stage of English acquisition the child is in. The four general phases of second language acquisition are described in Chapter 5 and should be taken into consideration during language interactions and interactive reading activities. (See following list.)

   a. If the child is still primarily *using his or her home language* to communicate, then the English version of the story may not be understood. For these children, it will be important for someone, a volunteer, parent, or older child to read the book to the child in his or her home language, in school or in the home by a family member. If possible, have the book read to the child in his or her home language prior to the English reading so the child will already understand the story and can follow along.

   b. If the child is in the *nonverbal or observational* stage, then you will want to prompt children with language that allows the child to point to objects or responses. ELL children in this stage may not be ready to "go public"

Dialogic Reading

Teachers actively engage children in the reading process by using the PEER sequence:

P   Prompting the child to comment on the book
E   Evaluating the child's response
E   Expanding the child's response
R   Repeating the prompt and checking for understanding

with their new language—but may have an extensive receptive vocabulary that they can demonstrate nonverbally. During this stage, the child should not be pressured to respond with English—but given lots of opportunities to listen and respond non-verbally.

   c. If the child is just beginning to use English in *telegraphic or formulaic speech* (i.e., children are just beginning to use common phrases like *I wanna*, and repeat syllables and words that they may not completely understand), then you will want to ask "what, where, when" questions that do not demand complex language use. Children may repeat "high-function" phrases often, even when they are not conversationally appropriate. During this stage, use verbal prompts such as the following: "What did the boy find? Where did the family go? "Goldilocks ate the _____ [child is prompted with the teacher's pause to fill in by saying 'porridge'], and it was _____ [child is prompted to fill in the missing word by saying 'cold']." In these examples, the child is asked to use familiar vocabulary but not complex grammar that he or she has not yet mastered.

   d. As the child becomes more fluent and moves into the *productive language stage*, you will want to increase the linguistic demands in English and ask open-ended recall questions that require more academic and decontextualized language. As with any intentional teaching, it is important for you to continuously assess the child's abilities, adapt the teaching expectations as you observe emerging abilities, and increase the language demands as the child becomes more capable.

13. After reading a book to ELL children, provide opportunities to use the new vocabulary, make connections between their own life and the text, and extend the early literacy skills to other areas of the curriculum. It is also important to explicitly promote phonological awareness, alphabet knowledge, and knowledge of print during the reading lessons. For ELL children, these skills can be taught in either their home language, especially if the home language is alphabetic like Spanish, or in English. These are skills that, once learned in any language, will transfer to a second language. So, if you are reading a book in Spanish, you can point out the letters of the Spanish alphabet, help the child to sound out Spanish words, and sing rhyming songs in Spanish with the knowledge that the children will apply these literacy skills to English reading. Once children know these early literacy skills, they can apply them to the English language!

Question: How might you adapt your instruction for a child who was in the very beginning stage of English acquisition?

ASSESSMENT APPROACHES: HOW TO COLLECT ACCURATE INFORMATION ON THE DEVELOPMENT OF DUAL LANGUAGE LEARNERS

Conducting accurate, systematic, and meaningful assessments can provide key insights into the development and emerging abilities of our children, thus providing the basis of effective individualized instruction. In general, early childhood professionals follow the set of *Principles and Recommendations for Early Childhood Assessments*, developed by The National Education Goals Panel (Shepard, Kagan, & Wurtz, 1998) which identified four broad purposes for early childhood assessments:

1. to promote learning and development of individual children;
2. to identify children with special needs and health conditions for intervention purposes;
3. to monitor trends in programs and evaluate program effectiveness; and
4. to obtain benchmark data for accountability purposes at the local, state, and national levels.

As the children and families we serve become increasingly diverse culturally, linguistically, ethnically, and economically, it is important to remember that all assessment procedures and instruments carry the potential for bias. This is especially true when teachers and children do not share the same cultural and linguistic background. For example, if a young girl from Taiwan enters a preschool program and the teacher does not understand her language or customs, how is the teacher able to accurately rate her social competence? If the young girl never responds to a social initiative by an adult and avoids contact with boys, but cheerfully watches out for younger children from her neighborhood, would the teacher understand the girl's social strengths and rate her accurately? Or if this same child can recognize five Chinese characters, but no letters of the English language alphabet, is she developing age-appropriate early literacy skills? Without knowing how our curriculum goals and expectations are translated and reflected in different and often culturally specific patterns of behavior, this teacher may underestimate the social and academic competencies of this young girl.

Even authentic and direct assessment information such as classroom observations of children's behavior can reflect mainstream biases when school personnel do not understand the cultural background and home languages of the children. This underscores the need for school personnel to reach out to families and increase their understanding of diverse family values, customs, and expectations for behavior. Increased understanding of culturally specific patterns of behavior that demonstrate developmental progress is essential for the early childhood workforce; it also highlights the need to aggressively recruit and train a more diverse workforce including ECE professionals at all levels—not just paraprofessionals. In order to accurately assess all children it will be critical for administrators, supervisors, psychologists, support specialists, as well as teachers and assistants to both reflect the culture and languages of the children they serve as well as possess the teaching knowledge and skills to understand when specific adaptations are needed for children from diverse backgrounds.

However, to meet the demands of program accountability and child assessment, the following recommendations are offered for young ELLs:

• Assessors need to understand the process and stages of acquiring a second language so they can accurately interpret the language proficiency of an emergent bilingual child, both in English and in the child's home language.

• The child's early language experiences, with particular attention to home language learning opportunities, must be considered when assessing oral language proficiency. Bilingualism may result in a slower rate of vocabulary development than children learning a single language. As children are acquiring two languages and becoming bilingual, one language may dominate. This is normal. It does not mean that the child is necessarily language delayed or disordered. Results of any vocabulary test or other similar assessment must be interpreted with caution if the child is a preschool-age or primary-grade ELL child and must be done within the context of the information on the child's early language experiences.

- The child must be assessed in the home language as well as in English. Knowing how the child is progressing in the home language is important for long-term academic success and educational planning. When assessment instruments are not available in the child's home language, multiple assessment methods (i.e., observation of child in different contexts, direct child assessments, informal language interactions with teachers and other adults) combined with information from parents can provide insights about the child's age-appropriate language abilities. It may not be possible to precisely know each ELL child's level of home language proficiency, but by using a variety of methods and assessors, teachers can make good estimates of home language abilities.

- Parents and other family members must be included in the assessment process. With the help of translators, if necessary, parents can share information about the child's language competence with siblings, peers, parents, and other adults.

- It is recommended that all children who speak a language other than English in the home receive an *individualized language plan* (ILP). (See Appendix D for an example.) This ILP should contain information from multiple sources about the child's current language competence in the home language as well as English and identify specific instructional goals that capitalize on the child's functional strengths. The ILP should also include strategies for including family activities and community resources whenever possible. For instance, if the child appears somewhat delayed in productive language ability in the home language and is just entering a preschool setting, the immediate priority may be to strengthen the home language learning opportunities through a combination of family interactions and community assistance. For this child, because the first language is not well developed, it may indicate a slower exposure to a second language (English) and more intensive home language support.

- Assessment information should be frequently collected and reviewed by all the teaching staff to monitor changes in language and overall development. There should be regular staff meetings (weekly if possible, at least monthly) that focus on careful analysis of assessment information and instructional activities should be adjusted accordingly.

- Classroom assessment activities should be frequent, include multiple procedures, and reflect the goals of the program's curriculum. This type of assessment should be ongoing and repeatedly capture information on what skills and abilities (and in which languages) children demonstrate in natural settings.

The matrix in Table 6.1 offers suggested procedures for gathering information about different aspects of language development for children who are ELLs.

Teachers can gain information about a child's language abilities through focused one-on-one interactions.

TABLE 6.1 Matrix for the Language/Literacy Assessment of Young ELL Children

Purpose for assessment	Types of measures/procedures
Determination of language dominance	☐ Parent/Family Survey with questions about language use, interaction patterns, and language proficiency ☐ Teacher observation of language usage across multiple contexts ☐ Possible use of English language screener
Language proficiency	☐ Language samples across multiple settings ☐ Standardized language measures of receptive and productive capacity used cautiously, i.e., Woodcock-Munoz Language Survey (WMLS); Expressive One-Word Picture Vocabulary Test (EOWPVT) and Receptive One-Word Picture Vocabulary Test (ROWPVT) ☐ Teacher ratings and/or observations
Language outcomes	☐ Informal assessments aligned with curriculum goals in language of instruction ☐ Language narrative samples in home language and English ☐ Standardized tests in English and home language (see examples of tests in previous row)

Source: Data from *Assessing Young English Language Learners for Developmental Outcomes,* commissioned paper for the National Academies of Science Committee on Child Assessment and Outcomes, by L. Espinosa, 2008a, Washington, DC: National Academies Press.

PUTTING IT ALL TOGETHER: ECE SETTINGS WHERE ELL CHILDREN CAN FLOURISH

As in high-quality early childhood teaching for all children, early education for young ELL children needs to be intentional, based on extensive knowledge of the children's background and prior knowledge, infused with respect for the home language and cultural values, and combined with continuous assessment procedures. Intentional teaching for ELL children begins with explicit language and literacy goals that identify and build on home language strengths while systematically introducing the children to all aspects of the English language. It also includes a comprehensive curriculum that reflects the principles of a high-quality intentional preschool curriculum (see box below) (National Association for the Education of Young Children [NAEYC] and the National Association of Early Childhood Specialists in State Departments of Education [NAECS/SDE], 2003).

In addition, at a symposium hosted by the National Center for Children in Poverty, which focused on the essential conditions for success for young children living in poverty, the participants identified the following characteristics of a high-quality intentional curriculum (Klein & Knitzer, 2006):

- is research based;
- emphasizes teachers actively engaging with children;
- includes attention to social and self-regulation skills;
- is responsive to cultural diversity and ELLs;
- is not teacher proof—allows for teacher judgment and knowledge to influence content and pacing; and
- requires new ways that are culturally and linguistically sensitive to measure classroom quality, teacher effectiveness, and student progress.

The intentional teaching strategies for young ELL children will look similar to high-quality instruction for all young children, but will include specific adaptations and enhancements for children whose home language is not English. During all

---

Joint Position Statement on Curriculum (NAEYC/NAECS/SDE)

Policy makers, the early childhood profession, and other stakeholders in young children's lives have a shared responsibility to implement a curriculum that is

- thoughtfully planned,
- challenging,
- engaging,
- developmentally appropriate,
- culturally and linguistic responsive,
- comprehensive across all developmental domains, and
- likely to promote positive outcomes for all young children.

Source: Early Childhood Curriculum, Assessment, and Program Evaluation: Building an Effective, Accountable System in Programs for Young Children Birth Through Age 8, a joint position statement by NAEYC and NAECS/SDE, 2003, Washington, DC: NAEYC.

parts of the daily schedule—arrival, circle time, choice time, snack time and lunchtime, small group/direct instruction, transitions, outdoor time, and pickup/departure—children's home language and cultural knowledge will be used as resources and as the foundation for building dual language competency.

Summary

The latest research and program evaluations are helping us to answer the question, What exactly does it mean to provide linguistically appropriate instruction to young ELLs? Although we do not know all the answers, the available evidence does lead to certain recommendations. Early childhood educators need to make specific instructional adaptations for ELL children: support for the child's home language leads to the best long-term growth and development; as much individualization and small-group instruction as possible; incorporating and building on each child's prior knowledge, frequent and continuous monitoring of the child's stage of language development; and finally, a general, high-quality, intentional curriculum. The strategies described in this chapter offer concrete approaches to lessons consistent with the research and easy to implement. These recommendations are not meant to be exhaustive—but a beginning point. As we all become better informed about how to promote long-term achievement for young ELL children, creative teachers and curriculum developers will surely add to this volume. These basic principles derived from research can be used to guide specific decision making. For it is in the day-to-day, minute-to-minute decisions that teachers make about when to respond, how to respond, which language to use, who to include, and how to judge progress that will determine the educational fate of ELL children.

Reflection and Discussion Questions

1. How many different languages do you speak? If you speak more than one language, at what age did you learn the second language? What do you remember about learning a second language?

2. How would you know if a young ELL child understood basic concepts like *fast, bigger than, up, down,* and so on, if they knew them only in Mandarin, a language you do not understand?

3. How might you proceed if you suspected that a child from Thailand who had just recently enrolled in your program had very limited home language abilities? Who would you contact and what resources might you use?

4. Describe one curricular adaptation described in this chapter that you could try out with an ELL child. What music, video, or book materials might help you with this adaptation?

Meeting the Future Challenges of Early Childhood Education

The future of any society depends on its ability to foster the health and well-being of the next generation. Stated simply, today's children will become tomorrow's citizens, workers, and parents. When we invest wisely in children and families, the next generation will pay that back through a lifetime of productivity and responsible citizenship. When we fail to provide children with what they need to build a strong foundation for healthy and productive lives, we put our future prosperity and security at risk.

NATIONAL SCIENTIFIC COUNCIL ON THE DEVELOPING CHILD, 2007a

The scientific community as well as many prominent economists and policy makers are all calling for expanded investments in high-quality early childhood programs. Among educators and researchers, a national consensus is building around early education. "Considerable evidence now supports the conclusion that high quality infant/toddler programs, pre-K [prekindergarten] programs, and K–3 schooling can contribute to meaningfully higher levels of school readiness and school achievement among low-SES students, including low-SES Hispanics" (National Task Force on Early Childhood Education for Hispanics, 2007, p. 46). In fact, James Heckman, Nobel Prize winner in economics, and Dimitry

Masterov have argued in their manuscript, *The Productivity Argument for Investing in Young Children* (2007) that "[t]he best way to improve the American workforce of the 21st century is to invest in early education to ensure that even the most disadvantaged children have the opportunity to succeed alongside their more advantaged peers" (p. 3). They further state the following:

> *Ability gaps between disadvantaged and other children open up early, before schooling begins. Conventional school-based policies start too late to completely remedy early deficits, although they can do some good. Children who start ahead keep accelerating past their peers, widening the gap.*
>
> *Learning begets learning and skill begets skill. Early advantages accumulate, so do early disadvantages.*
>
> *Returns are highest for investments made at younger ages and remedial investments are often prohibitively costly.*
>
> *The best way to improve the schools is to improve the early environments of the children sent to them. (Heckman & Masterov, 2007, p. 2)*

Whether you are looking at early childhood education from an economic, educational, or moral perspective, there are compelling arguments to expand, enhance, and carefully monitor high-quality early education for this nation's young children—particularly those from low-SES, non-English-speaking, and/or culturally diverse homes. As outlined in Chapter 2, this recognition of the importance of the early years and the wisdom of investing in early childhood has led to growth in funding for program expansion at all levels—city, county, state, and federal. More young children than at any point in our national history are receiving some form of out-of-home organized early care and education. However, these gains are fragile, vulnerable to reductions in economically uncertain times, and the practices are not necessarily based on the latest research. The *State of Preschool: 2008 State Preschool Yearbook* concluded, "[A]cross our nation, high-quality and readily available state-funded preschool programs are the exception rather than the rule" (Barnett et al., 2008, p. 4).

To create a stable, sustainable, and effective system we will need to do the following:

1. Bolster our national will and build consensus that investments in high-quality education for young children is in everyone's best interest.
2. Continuously conduct and incorporate rigorous research into our educational practices.
3. Link early childhood to national educational policies.
4. Advocate for sufficient resources to realize this vision.

NATIONAL WILL

Why hasn't the United States enacted policies ensuring that every preschool-aged child receives comprehensive health and high-quality educational programming? I believe that one aspect of our national culture is the American value of independence, the historic value of rugged individualism, and the sanctity of the nuclear family. Although these features of our cultural identity have been important features of our historical identity, they possess questionable validity in contemporary society and may actually fuel a resistance to public support for early intervention. Our task now is to balance the historical value of individualism with the need to expand early educational opportunities for *all* to promote the common good. Clearly, it will take leadership and a national commitment to these goals that is reinforced by state governments. This country needs to *believe* that every child deserves an opportunity to develop his full potential—that it is in all our interests to invest public resources in young children and that scientific research can guide the design of specific approaches.

One way to influence the national support for early education is to continue to hold public and private forums on the research base that clearly articulate the rationale from a scientific perspective. Careful, continuous, and persistent presentation of the arguments for expansion of early childhood education combined with examples of success can slowly chip away at preconceived biases and outmoded views. The Partnership for America's Economic Success (PAES) was created by a group of foundations, business leaders, economists, policy experts, and advocates to "lay the groundwork for making the success of every child the nation's top economic priority" (Partnership for America's Economic Success, 2008, p. 1). This organization is commissioning multidisciplinary research on the costs and benefits of investing in young children as well as innovative funding strategies. PAES will use this information to "identify and advance opportunities to encourage state and national policy makers to adopt policies that effectively invest in young children" (Partnership for America's Economic Success, 2008, p. 1). According to PAES, there are three phases to building this national agenda:

1. gathering the evidence of economic impact and laying the groundwork,
2. building coalitions and developing the policy agenda, and
3. expanding public education and advocacy to make children the top economic priority of the nation.

I would argue that the scientific and economic evidence is sufficient to move into phase two (Barnett, 2008; Isaacs, 2008; National Scientific Council on the Developing Child, 2007a, 2007b, 2007c, 2008). As additional philanthropic foundations make early investment a major focus (e.g., Gates Foundation, Buffett Foundation, Pew Charitable Trusts, and Robin Hood Foundation) and private initiatives partner with local and state government, communities will be better equipped to design funding strategies and program options that fit their populations and resources. The point is that we must first agree that we *can* successfully build programs for *all* young children and that we *must* invest now—our young children cannot wait. Each year that we delay means countless opportunities lost for our children, our families, and our country.

Early childhood educators can make important contributions to this effort by being familiar with the research recommendations outlined in this book and being willing to communicate these points at parent and community meetings. Each one of us can be a persuasive voice for the importance of high-quality early education within our programs and communities. The knowledge based on solid scientific research that you have, combined with your commitment to young children and families, will help to convince parents and administrators that we now know enough to improve practices and *get it right.*

USING RESEARCH, ADVOCACY, AND PERSISTENCE TO MOVE THE AGENDA FORWARD: INCH-BY-INCH, STEP-BY-STEP

The process of moving forward on a local or national agenda for early childhood cannot be viewed as a linear, steady march to full implementation. It will require concerted effort over time and persistence in the face of intermittent setbacks. In their classic book on early childhood advocacy, Stacy Goffin and Joan Lombardi (1989) argue that all early educators have the professional and ethical responsibility to advocate on behalf of young children, who often have no voice. They identified six strategies that will help early childhood professionals realize their commitment to children:

1. sharing our knowledge,
2. sharing our professional experiences,
3. redefining the "bottom line" for children,
4. standing up for our profession,
5. activating parental power, and
6. expanding the constituency for children (pp. 11–14).

A recent book by Judith Kieff, *Informed Advocacy in Early Childhood Care and Education: Making a Difference for Young Children and Families* (2008), reaffirms these principles and expands on the different contexts for advocacy beginning locally and working outward to global advocacy. In addition, Pre-K Now, a public education and advocacy organization funded by the Pew Charitable Trust (see Web site at http://www.preknow.org), provides facts, current research findings, presentations, and opportunities for collegial dialogue for prekindergarten advocates. One thing all early childhood organizations agree on is the need for advocates to be well informed with the latest information that is not distorted or exaggerated.

As many of us who have been working on these issues for decades know, transformations in the national or local will not come quickly, easily, or cheaply. It takes all of us working consistently in whatever forums we have available to us to move this agenda forward. We must all stay informed, stand together, and use our personal and professional capital wisely. Within our profession, we need to agree on the big issues and try not to splinter into opposing camps over the details. The abundance of credible scientific research from multiple sectors does provide an advantage that has only recently become available. The following examples offer reassurance that our efforts can be successful at both the local program and state levels:

The early childhood profession is demonstrating that little-by-little, step-by-step informed educators and advocates can help to reshape the landscape for our youngest citizens. Certainly we will not be persuasive with every audience

---

State Education Officials Do Listen and Respond to Research

Several years ago while I was actively researching the impacts of different early education approaches on educational achievement testing for ELLs, a state department of education with a rapidly increasing ELL population asked me to present a two-hour overview of the research. They were concerned about the high dropout rates and low achievement levels of their growing numbers of children who spoke Spanish in the home. They recognized that to meet the Average Yearly Progress (AYP) requirements of No Child Left Behind (NCLB), they needed to improve the educational progress of ELL children.

Viewing this as a great opportunity, I organized my data and findings into a two-hour slide show. I was not too optimistic because this state had shown little interest in preschool and even less interest in changing their policies toward ELLs. After about an hour of my presentation of data, the president of the state board stopped me and said, "This is all very interesting, but what are the policy implications? We have heard a lot of data, but what does this mean for us—we are a state board of education that makes policy."

Another board member jumped in. "I know what this means. We need to have preschool for all—and make them all bilingual preschools. She is convincing me that all children will benefit from bilingual preschools."

Imagine my surprise, as this was not what I was recommending, but certainly a defensible conclusion. When I tried to clarify the research, I was stopped from continuing my presentation. The board wanted to talk among themselves about how they could increase their funding for preschool and recruit staff to make them all bilingual!

Although the state officials did not immediately follow through on these recommendations, they did measurably increase their funding for early childhood programs and created new positions for dual language professional development specialists. I was impressed with the eagerness of the state education department to understand new approaches that would work for ELL students and their ability to translate this information to state policies. This experience reaffirmed for me the need to be prepared to offer pragmatic, evidence-based solutions to pressing problems.

At all levels, educators are searching for guidance on how to improve their practices and policies for diverse children. Early childhood educators have the potential to influence this process.

---

or even be welcomed in some corridors of power, but through persistence, combined with well-developed arguments, we will make progress. One thing I have learned over the years is to not take rebuffs personally. When public officials or sometimes even your own colleagues dismiss your perspective, it does not mean they are rejecting you personally. They are simply not ready to hear what you have to say. On these topics of why there is such a high school failure rate for children who are living in poverty or those who do not understand English, many of us have strong feelings that interfere with rational consideration of the evidence. That is to be expected. Over time, with ongoing opportunities to digest new facts, most educators will reach fair and informed conclusions.

Early Childhood Teachers Can Influence Local Policy Makers

A school board member unexpectedly visited a kindergarten classroom in a prekindergarten through Grade 2 program that I supervised. The board member appeared surprised when he observed the children making long chains through the classroom and out into the hallways with math manipulatives and conversing among themselves—in Spanish and English. The children were making patterns of red and blue math blocks and talking about what color goes next, how many they had laid out, and where the rest of the blocks were.

The school board member asked the teacher why the children weren't studying their math facts and how was this activity going to help them master the district curriculum and pass the English achievement tests in first grade. He also seemed concerned about the use of Spanish. The kindergarten teacher explained that the children were highly motivated, focused on this lesson, and learning about number operations from the direct manipulation of objects. The children were also learning from one another as they discussed the pattern and the colors in the chain of blocks. Many of the children were in the early stages of English development and needed to communicate in their dominant language. She stressed the importance of learning the math concepts in any language.

This kindergarten teacher then went on to describe the latest results from our school achievement tests. All of our children, even our ELL children, had scored above average in the problem solving and reasoning sections of Grade 2 state tests. This teacher was knowledgeable about the methods she was using as well as the performance of the children. Her spirited explanation of her methods and their effectiveness seemed to convince this skeptical school board member. At the next board meeting, he remarked he had visited our program and "was very impressed by the teachers and what they were doing with the children."

LINK TO NATIONAL EDUCATION PRIORITIES AND POLICIES

While working in public school systems throughout the states of Washington and California, I learned that in order to be heard, I had to link the early childhood goals to larger district priorities. Many administrators and policy makers do not understand how the well-being of small children before they can read or write is directly related to district standardized test scores and high school graduation rates. All schools are focused on meeting their AYP goals that must be reported under the NCLB. According to this legislation, "Adequate yearly progress is the minimum level of improvement that states, school districts, and schools must achieve each year, according to federal . . . NCLB . . . legislation. This progress is determined by a collection of performance measures that a state, its school districts, and subpopulations of students within its schools are supposed to meet if the state receives Title I federal funding." (See http://www.schoolwisepress.com/smart/dict/dict.html for more detailed information about AYP.) All students, including ELLs, must be assessed annually and must show progress in both English proficiency and academic achievement across subjects.

The incremental yearly progress is assessed with standardized measurements in math and reading/language arts beginning in third grade. School districts must be able to show that by the year 2014 all students in all subgroups (including children in poverty, ELL students, and those with special needs) will be proficient in language arts and math. These external demands for school accountability have created pressure for school officials to ensure that *all* of their students are learning important academic content and master grade expectations.

As professionals working with young children, we must be able to persuasively demonstrate how the quality of our programs will directly impact the achievement of larger district goals. At times in my career, I have felt that my programs were the least well funded and considered marginal to the district mission. Most often, I had to fight just to keep our office and classroom space from being taken over by the school administration for other, "more important" programs. However, over the years, I learned that once the community and the district administration understood the vital linkages between what we accomplished with 3-year-olds and reducing dropout rates and improving achievement test scores among middle school students, it was easier to secure long-term commitments and stable funding for early childhood programs. All segments of the educational community need to understand that early intervention is not a luxury or a "fringe issue," but a critical component of long-term school success.

To accurately communicate the benefits of high-quality early education for children from diverse backgrounds, it is necessary for all of us to be knowledgeable about the research base—what it has found and what is still to be discovered. This does not mean that everyone needs to become a sophisticated scholar, but we all must be able to discuss the basic findings without exaggerating or distorting them. Many of the policy reports I have referenced in this book as well as the resources identified in Appendix B outline the scientific findings in more detail. The scientific rationale for designing programs for children who are from diverse backgrounds in particular ways also needs to be well understood. As early childhood educators, we will be working with professional educators who are not familiar with young children or with "best practices" for young ELL children, so we must be prepared to present the rationale for the strategies we implement. This book has outlined much of the scientific basis that underlies specific instructional strategies. Please read it, use it, and question it!

INVESTMENT: RESOURCES NEEDED

Early child development is economic development with a very high public return. I want to stress that it's a public return. I want to stress that it's an economic return.

Arthur J. Rolnick, Senior Vice President and Director of Research, Federal Reserve Bank of Minneapolis, 2006

Kids who have access to prekindergarten have a better chance to succeed in school, get into college, and get a good-paying job later in life. However, we also know that too many of our children begin school under-prepared. Instead of a head start in life, they're too often already a step behind. The achievement gap in our schools exists for many kids before they even start kindergarten.

New Mexico Governor Bill Richardson, 2006

According to the PAES Advisory Board chair, Robert Dugger (PAES, 2008),

> *Making the best use of every resource—human and financial—means we're going to have to agree on a set of core principles to guide all our spending decisions.*
>
> **1.** *U.S. spending choices will need to be based on evidence-based long-term economic returns.*
> **2.** *Policies and program will need to have measurable goals and draw on best practices.*
> **3.** *Performance evaluation will need to be built into programs and policies before they are funded. (PAES, 2008, Presentation to the National Economic Forum on Early Childhood Investment)*

Although it is difficult to accurately estimate the cost of making high-quality early education available for all children who choose to enroll, Helene Stebbens and Barbara Langford, two prominent early childhood advocates (2006), have identified three distinct cost categories and a five-step process to help state and community leaders develop effective financing strategies to support comprehensive services for young children. They recommend that agencies focus on (1) direct service costs, (2) infrastructure costs, and (3) capital costs. The five steps are as follows:

Step 1: Determine financing for what.

Step 2: Identify quality improvements.

Step 3: Create a cost model to determine the baseline cost estimate.

Step 4: Estimate the cost of improving quality.

Step 5: Determine ramp-up assumptions (Stebbens & Langford, 2006).

Using a cost–estimate framework and process like this will help leaders engage in more accurate financial planning. The amount required will be substantial and viewed skeptically, especially during times of budget shortfalls; however, the cost of not making these investments may be even greater. This cannot be done cheaply. Quality is essential and quality costs. According to a recent analysis of state funding levels, 19 states spent enough on prekindergarten programs to meet minimum standards of quality (Barnett et al., 2008). The other 19 states that provide prekindergarten programs may or may not have sufficient resources for high quality, depending on the level of funding from local sources. The growing trend for states to offer more educational programs for preschool-aged children is welcome. However, more programs do not necessarily mean all programs will be of sufficient quality or designed to meet the needs of children from diverse backgrounds.

Currently, states use a variety of methods to determine the amount of public funding for prekindergarten programs. The amount spent varies from nothing (12 states) to more than $10,000 per child in New Jersey for preschool-aged children. Nationally, the average amount spent by states on prekindergarten programs was $3,642 per child (Barnett et al., 2008). The percentages of children served across the states also shows great disparities. Those states with UPK serve the highest percentages of preschool-aged children (e.g., Oklahoma, 68.4%; Florida, 56.7%; and Georgia, 53.3%). Children living in one of the 12 states with no public funding for prekindergarten have no programs (Barnett et al., 2008).

James Heckman, the Nobel Prize-winning economist from the University of Chicago, has estimated that effective early intervention will yield an estimated private net benefit to the participants of $102.4 billion and to the public of $409.2 billion, for a total benefit of over $511 billion in taxpayer, crime victimization, and employer costs. As we look to the future and envision a qualified workforce of competent adults, we simply cannot afford to not make these investments.

Summary

The urgent message of this book is fueled by a convergence of multiple influences: the demographic shifts rippling through rural and urban communities, creating new populations of children and families that require new approaches and strategies; the compelling research unveiled during the last two decades that provides scientific evidence of both the need to intervene early and the guidance on how to design effective programs for diverse families and learners; and the ethical obligation to address significant discrepancies in opportunity to learn. As the National Scientific Council on the Developing Child (2007b) stated,

> [T]he time has come to begin to close the gap between what we know (from systematic scientific inquiry across a broad range of disciplines) and what we do (through both public and private sector policies and practices) to promote the healthy development of all young children. The need to address significant inequalities in opportunity, beginning in the earliest years of life, is both a fundamental moral responsibility and a critical investment in our nation's social and economic future. As such, it is a compelling task that calls for broad, bipartisan collaboration. (p. 13)

Reflection and Discussion Questions

1. What kind of support have you observed in your community for high-quality early education?
2. Have you ever considered yourself an advocate for early childhood education? How would you need to prepare yourself to advocate on behalf of young children from diverse backgrounds?
3. What arguments have you heard in your community for or against expanding early childhood services to all children? How would you respond to the following statement: "We just can't afford to expand our programs and serve more children."

APPENDIX A

Sample Family Languages and Interests Survey

1. Who are the members of your family?
2. How old is your child?
3. Who is the primary caregiver of your child?
4. What language did your child learn when he or she first began to talk?
5. What language do you speak most often with your child?

   Only English..........Mostly English..........Two languages..........Mostly my primary language..........Only my primary language

6. What language does your child speak most frequently with you?

   Only English..........Mostly English..........Two languages..........Mostly my primary language..........Only my primary language

7. What language does your child speak most often with other children?

   Only English..........Mostly English..........Two languages..........Mostly my primary language..........Only my primary language

8. What special talents or interests does your child have?
9. Who does your child play with most often?
10. What are your aspirations for your child?
11. What are your expectations for your child's school?
12. Do you have any hobbies or interests that you would like to share with your child's class?
13. What are your feelings about your child learning English? How do you feel about your child continuing to use your home language?

APPENDIX B

Resources for Serving Young Children from Diverse Backgrounds

WEB SITES

- Acquiring English as a Second Language: What's Normal What's Not. http://www.asha.org/public/speech/development/easl.htm
- Bilingual Acquisition by Fred Genesee. http://www.colorincolorado.org/article/12916?theme=print
- California Association for Bilingual Education. http://www.bilingualeducation.org
- California Tomorrow (provides resources for working with children, parents and other adults on culture and language). http://www.californiatomorrow.org
- Challenging Common Myths About Young English Learners, by Linda Espinosa, Foundation for Child Development. http://www.fcd-us.org/resources/resources_show.htm?doc_id=669789
- CLAS (Culturally and Linguistically Appropriate Services) Early Childhood Research Institute. Review Guidelines for material selection: Child assessment. http://www.clas.uiuc.edu/review/RG-ChildAssessment.html
- Collins, R., & Ribeiro, R. (2004). Toward an early care and education agenda for Hispanic children. http://www.ecrp.uiuc.edu/v6n2/collins.html
- Colorín, Colorado (a bilingual site for families and educators of English learners). http://www.colorincolorado.org/
- Cooperative Children's Book Center, School of Education, University of Wisconsin—Madison: Multicultural Books. http://www.education.wisc.edu/ccbc/books/detailLists.asp?idBookListCat=1
- Espinosa, L. (2008). *Challenging common myths about young English language learners*. Foundation for Child Development Policy Brief No. Eight. http://www.fcd-us.org/resources/resources_show.htm?doc_id=669789
- Expanding and Improving Early Education for Hispanics, Main Report of the National Task Force on Early Childhood Education for Hispanics, Para Nuestros Niños Web site http://www.ecehispanic.org
- Hepburn, K. S. (2004). Building culturally and linguistically competent services to support young children, their families, and school readiness. http://www.aecf.org/KnowledgeCenter/Publications.aspx?pubguid={6F04722C-85EB-45BF-B6B3-07FFF5E435A9}
- Journal of the National Association for the Education of Young Children: Resources on Embracing Diversity in Early Childhood Settings. http://www.journal.naeyc.org/btj/200511/DiversityResourcesBTJ1105.asp
- Learning Two Languages, American Speech-Language-Hearing Association (available in Spanish and as a brochure). http://www.asha.org/public/speech/development/BilingualChildren.htm

- Making a Difference: A Framework for Supporting First and Second Language Development in Preschool Children of Migrant Farmworkers, Academy for Education Development. http://www.aed.org/Publications/loader.cfm?url=/commonspot/security/getfile.cfm&pageid=3352
- National Association for the Education of Young Children. (2005). Screening and assessment of young English-language learners. http://www.naeyc.org/about/jobs/overview
- National Clearinghouse for English Language Acquisition. (2006). *Resources About Early Childhood Education.* Washington, DC. http://www.ncela.gwu.edu/resabout/ecell/index.html
- National Institute for Early Education Research, Research Topic of English Language Learners. http://nieer.org/research/topic.php?TopicID=4
- Reading is Fundamental: Bilingual Children's Books. http://www.rif.org/educators/books/Bilingual_books.mspx
- Reading is Fundamental: Bilingual Versions of Popular Children's Books. http://www.rif.org/educators/books/Bilingual_versions.mspx
- Reading is Fundamental: 100 of the Decade's Best Multicultural Read-Alouds, Pre-kindergarten through Grade 8, selected and annotated by Judy Freeman. http://www.rif.org/educators/books/100_best_multicultural.mspx
- Reading is Fundamental: Wordless and Almost Wordless Picture Books. http://www.rif.org/educators/books/Picture-Books.mspx
- RealeWriter. http://www.realebooks.com
- Santos, R. M., & Reese, D. (1999). Selecting culturally and linguistically appropriate materials: Suggestions for service providers. http://ceep.crc.uiuc.edu/eecearchive/digests/1999/santos99.pdf
- The Early Authors Program by Judith K. Bernhard et al. www.ryerson.ca/~bernhard/early.html

BOOKS AND ARTICLES

Akaran, S. E., & Fields, M. V. (1997). Family and cultural context: A writing break-through? *Young Children, 52* (4), 37–40.

Bisson, J. (1997). *Celebrate! An anti-bias guide to enjoying holidays in early child-hood programs.* St. Paul, MN: Redleaf.

Bredekamp, S. (2003). Resolving contradictions between cultural practices. In Copple, C. (Ed.), *A world of difference.* Washington, DC: National Association for the Education of Young Children.

Brown, J. C., & Oates, L. A. (Eds.). (2001). *Books to grow on: African American lit-erature for young children* [Brochure]. Washington, DC: National Association for the Education of Young Children.

Brown, K., Fitzpatrick, T. S., & Morrison, G. S. (2004). Valuing diversity in class-rooms through family involvement. *Dimensions of Early Childhood, 3,* 11–18.

Bruns, D. A., & Corso, R. M. (2001). *Working with culturally and linguistically di-verse families.* Champaign, IL: ERIC Clearinghouse on Elementary and Early Childhood Education. (EDO-PS-01-4.)

Byrnes, D. A., & Kiger, G. (Eds.). (2005). *Common bonds: Anti-bias teaching in a diverse society* (3rd ed.). Olney, MD: Association for Childhood Education International.

Chang, H. N.-L., Femeneall, T., Louise, N., Murdock, B., & Pell, E. (2000). *Walking the walk: Principles for building community capacity for equity and diversity.* Oakland: California Tomorrow.

Copple, C. (Ed.). (2003). *A world of difference: Readings on teaching young children in a diverse society.* Washington, DC: National Association for the Education of Young Children.

Derman-Sparks, L. (1999). Markers of multicultural/anti-bias education. *Young Children, 54* (5), 43.

Derman-Sparks, L., & the A.B.C. Task Force. (1989). *Anti-bias curriculum: Tools for empowering young children.* Washington, DC: National Association for the Education of Young Children.

Derman-Sparks, L., & Ramsey, P. G. (2006). *What if all the kids are white? Engaging white children and their families in anti-bias/multicultural education.* New York: Teachers College Press.

Duarte, G., & Gutierrez, C. (2004). Best practices in bilingual early childhood classrooms. *NABE News, 27* (4), 4–7.

Espinosa, L. (2006). Curriculum and assessment considerations for young children from culturally, linguistically, and economically diverse backgrounds. *Psychology in the Schools 42* (8), 837–854.

Espinosa, L. (2007). English-language learners as they enter school. In Pianta, R. & Snow, K. (Eds.), *School readiness, early learning, and the transition to school* (pp. 175–196). Baltimore, MD: Paul H Brookes.

Espinosa, L. (2008). Early literacy for English language learners. In A. DeBruin-Parecki (Ed.), *Effective early literacy practice.* Baltimore, MD: Brookes Publishing.

Fassler, R. (2003). *Room for talk: Teaching and learning in a multilingual kindergarten.* New York: Teachers College Press.

Gartrell, D. (2004). *The power of guidance: Teaching social-emotional skills in early childhood.* Washington, DC: National Association for the Education of Young Children; Clifton Park, NY: Delmar Learning.

Genishi, C. (2002). Young English language learners: Resourceful in the classroom [Research in Review]. *Young Children, 57* (4), 66–70.

Hickman-Davis, P. (2002). "Cuándo no hablan Inglés": Helping young children learn English as a second language. *Dimensions of Early Childhood, 2,* 3–10.

Houk, F. A. (2005). *Supporting English language learners: A guide for teachers and administrators.* Portsmouth, NH: Heinemann.

Jacobsen, T. (2003). *Confronting our discomfort: Clearing the way for anti-bias in early childhood.* Portsmouth, NH: Heinemann.

Kaufman, H. (2001). Skills for working with all families. *Young Children, 56* (4), 81–83.

Ladson-Billings, G. (1994). *The dreamkeepers: Successful teachers of African American children.* San Francisco: Jossey-Bass.

Martinez, F. (2005). Early care and education for Hispanic children. *Childhood Education, 81* (3), 174–176.

Meier, D. R. (2004). *The young child's memory for words: Developing first and second language and literacy.* New York: Teachers College Press.

Moomaw, S. (2002). *Nobody else like me: Activities to celebrate diversity.* St. Paul, MN: Redleaf.

Quintero, E. (2004). Will I lose a tooth? Will I learn to read? Problem-posing with multicultural children's literature. *Young Children, 59* (3), 56–62.

Ramsey, P. G. (2004). *Teaching and learning in a diverse world: Multicultural education for young children* (3rd ed.). New York: Teachers College Press.

Riojas-Cortez, M., Flores, B., & Clark, E. (2003). Los niños aprenden en casa: Valuing and connecting home cultural knowledge with an early childhood program. *Young Children, 58* (6), 78–83.

Santos, R. M. (2004). Ensuring culturally and linguistically appropriate assessment of young children. *Young Children, 59*1, 48–50.

Santos, R. M., Corso, R. M., & Fowler, S. A. (Eds.). (2005). *Language and communication: Working with linguistically diverse families.* CLAS Collection #3. Longmont, CO: Sopris West.

Schon, I. (2002). *Books to grow on: Latino literature for young children* [Brochure]. Washington, DC: National Association for the Education of Young Children.

Schwartz, W. (1995). *A guide to communicating with Asian American families: For parents/About parents.* New York: ERIC Clearinghouse on Urban Education. ED 396014.

Some, S. (2000). *The spirit of intimacy: Ancient African teachings in the ways of relationships.* New York: HarperCollins/Quill.

Tabors, P. O. (1998). What early childhood educators need to know: Developing effective programs for linguistically and culturally diverse children and families. *Young Children, 53* (6), 20–26.

Tan, A. L. (2004). *Chinese American children and families: A guide for educators and service providers.* Olney, MD: Association for Childhood Education International.

MULTIMEDIA RESOURCES

Pinnegar, S., Teemant, A., & Tyra, S. (2002). *The early childhood literacy case: A video ethnography of balanced literacy approaches for second language students* [CD-ROM]. Center for Research on Education, Diversity, and Excellence (CREDE).

Tharp, R., Galarza, S., & Entz, S. (2002). *The Sheri Galarza Preschool case: A video ethnography of developmentally appropriate teaching of language and literacy* [CD-ROM]. Center for Research on Education, Diversity, and Excellence (CREDE).

A World Full of Language, Supporting Preschool English Learners (DVD). Available in Spanish and English from the California State Department of Education, Child Development Division. http://www.cde.ca.gov/re/pn/rc

APPENDIX C

Information on the Early Authors Program

The Early Authors Program (EAP) represents an innovative, effective means of supporting young children's literacy. The approach was piloted in Miami-Dade County, one of the nation's most diverse urban communities in 2003 to 2004. It was designed to help address poverty and illiteracy among Miami's culturally diverse population and to help close the achievement gap (Bernhard et al., 2004). The EAP was designed in collaboration with Alma Flor Ada and Isabel Campoy and based on the principles outlined in their book, *Authors in the Classroom* (2004). The authors believe that by encouraging young children to write, illustrate, and publish their own personal narratives jointly with their parents and teachers, we can nourish children's sense of self-worth and identity as readers and writers.

Each EAP classroom had a publishing station with a computer, printer, digital camera, and laminating machine. Initially, parents and teachers wrote about their own life experiences and shared them with the children. After a community of authors was established in the classrooms, the teachers began by taking pictures of the children engaged in favorite activities and scanning in family photos supplied by the parents. The children then narrated stories from the pictures and teachers typed the words onto the computers. If the child spoke a language other than English in the home, a bilingual version of the book was made.

The teachers then printed, laminated, and bound the pages into books that were shared in the school and taken home. The stories were about the children's own experiences, families, and classmates with titles such as *I Can . . . The Story of My Name . . . My Family,* and so on. Through the process of dictating, transcribing, and publishing, the children began to see the connection between speech and print. The evaluation of the EAP concluded, "[T]he present study provides strong support for the efficacy of the EAP with low-income, diverse preschoolers in a large, subsidized child care setting" (Bernhard et al., 2004, p. 30).

APPENDIX D

Sample Individualized Language Plan

Family Name_____ Date_____

Child's Name_____ DOB_____

I. Family Information

Who is part of your family? _____

What things do you like to do as a family?_____

What are your strengths as a family? _____

II. Results of Family Languages and Interests Survey (Appendix A)

III. Child Abilities, Strengths, Needs

Assessment Results

Observational Assessments (context, dates, and times, language[s] spoken, conversational partners) _____

_____

_____

_____

Standardized Assessments (measure[s] used, assessor, dates, and results) _____

_____

_____

_____

Parent Assessment of Child's Language Abilities _____

_____

_____

_____

Child Language Strengths/Needs in Home Language _____

_____

_____

_____

Child Language Strengths/Needs in English _____

_____

_____

_____

IV. Language Goals

Home language goals

1.

2.

3.

Resources Needed
In School (Who, What, When)

Out of School (Referrals)

English language goals

1.

2.

3.

Resources Needed
In School (Who, What, When)

Specific Strategies, Activities, Staff

Out of School (Referrals)

V. Monitoring of Progress

Evidence of progress, Who What, When (assessments, achievements, reports)

GLOSSARY

Achievement Gap. The achievement gap refers to the observed disparity on a number of educational measures between the performance of groups of students, especially groups defined by gender, race/ethnicity, and socioeconomic status. The achievement gap can be observed on a variety of measures, including standardized test scores, grade point average, dropout rates, and college-enrollment and -completion rates. Across the United States, a gap in academic achievement persists between minority and economically disadvantaged students and their White counterparts.

Assessment. A term often used loosely to refer to any type of information about young children's performance or competence. In a narrower sense, assessment refers to information from multiple indicators and sources of evidence that is organized, interpreted, and then evaluated to make a judgment about a child (Snow & Van Hemel, 2008).

Code Switching (mixing). The use of elements from two or more languages in the same utterance or in the same stretch of conversation.

Culture. A shared, learned symbolic system of values, beliefs, and attitudes that shapes and influences perception and behavior; in essence, it is a lens through which each of us views and interprets the world (Lynch & Hanson, 2004). Cultural understandings set out the expectations, rules, and guidelines of how to operate (live/act/behave) within a community.

Developmentally Appropriate Practice. Early childhood curriculum and teaching practices informed by what is known about child development and learning, what is known about each child as an individual, and what is known about the social and cultural contexts in which children live (adapted from National Association for the Education of Young Children, 1996, 2008).

Evidence-Based Practices (EBP). EBP usually refer to programs or practices that are proven to be successful through research methodology and have produced consistently positive patterns of results. EBPs or model programs that have shown the greatest levels of effectiveness are those that have established generalizability (repeated in different settings and with different populations over time) through research studies. The implementation of proven, well-researched programs, curricula, and approaches is rapidly becoming standard practice today and required by most funding sources.

Young English Language Learners/Dual Language Learners. Children whose first language is not English are often referred to as "English language learners (ELLs)." This definition includes those learning English for the first time in the preschool setting, as well as children who have developed various levels of English proficiency. Some states (e.g., California) use the term *English learners* (EL). Young ELLs are increasingly being referred to as *dual language learners*. A recent federal report defines dual language learners as young children, between 3 and 6 years of age, who are learning a second language while still developing basic competency in their first language (Ballantyne et al., 2008).

Language 1 (L1), Language 2 (L2). L1 refers to the first language spoken by a child, the language used in the child's home. This is the language through which the child has learned to process information, understand how language is structured, and interpret the world. L2 refers to the second language learned by the child. In the United States, L2 typically refers to English for children who are classified as ELLs.

Scientifically Based Research. Scientifically based research means the use of rigorous, systematic, and objective methodologies to obtain reliable and valid knowledge. Such research requires the use of logic, clear description of procedures and results, appropriate methods, collection of data and analysis, and some method of peer review. The term *scientifically based research* includes basic research, applied research, and evaluation research in which the rationale, design, and interpretation are developed in accordance with the scientific principles laid out above.

Socioeconomic Status (SES). A measure of an individual's or family's economic and social position relative to others, based on *income, education, and occupation.* When analyzing a family's SES, the household wage earner's education and occupation are examined, as well as combined income. Socioeconomic status is typically broken into three categories—high SES, middle SES, and low SES—to describe the three groups that can be applied to a family or individual. When placing a family or individual into one of these categories, any or all of the three variables (income, education, and occupation) can be assessed.

REFERENCES

Aber, J. L., Bennett, N. G., Conley, D. C., & Li, J. (2007). The effects of poverty on child health and development. *Annual Revue of Public Health, 18,* 463–483.

Ada, A. F., & Campoy, F. I. (2004). *Authors in the classroom: A transformative education process.* Boston: Allyn & Bacon.

Adams, M., Foorman, B., Lundberg, I., & Beeler, T. (1998). *Phonemic awareness in young children.* Baltimore: Brookes Publishing.

Alvarez, R., Barton, A., Clark, G., Keenan, J. F., Lalyre, Y., MacNeill, C., et al. (1992). *Young lives: Many languages, many cultures. Culturally & linguistically appropriate services.* Urbana–Champaign: Early Childhood Research Institute, University of Illinois at Urbana–Champaign.

American Library Association. (2004). *The Dialogic Reading Program for Parents of 2- and 3-Year-Olds.* Retrieved September 2008 from http://www.ala.org/ala/mgrps/divs/alsc/ecrr/researcha/researchbyagelevel/agetwotothree/agetwotothree.cfm

Arias, B., & Morillo-Campbell, M. (2008). *Promoting ELL parental involvement: Challenges in contested times.* Policy brief from Arizona State University, Education Policy Research Unit. Retrieved December 2008 from http://epsl.asu.edu/epru/documents/EPSL-0801-250-EPRU.pdf

Arnold, D. S., & Whitehurst, G. J. (1994). Accelerating language development through picture book reading: A summary of dialogic reading and its effect. In D. Dickinson (Ed.), *Bridges to literacy: Approaches supporting child and family literacy.* Cambridge, MA: Basil Blackwell.

Au, K. H. (1993). *Literacy instruction in multicultural settings.* New York: Harcourt Brace Publishing.

August, D. (2002). *Transitional programs for English language learners: Contextual factors and effective programming.* Baltimore: Center for Research on the Education of Students Placed at Risk.

August, D., & Hakuta, K. (Eds.). (1997). *Improving schooling for language-minority children: A research agenda.* Washington, DC: National Academy Press.

August, D., & Shanahan, T. (2006). *Developing literacy in second-language learners.* Report of the National Literacy Panel on Language Minority Children and Youth. Mahwah, NJ: Lawrence Erlbaum Publishers.

Ballantyne, K. G., Sandeerman, A. R., D'Emilio, T., & McLaughlin, N. (2008). *Dual language learners in the early years: Getting ready to succeed in school.* Washington, DC: National Clearinghouse for English Language Acquisition. Retrieved January 2009 from http://www.ncela.gwu.edu/resabout/ecell/earlyyears.pdf

Barnett, W. S. (2002). Early childhood education. In A. Molnar (Ed.), *School reform proposals: The research evidence.* Greenwich, CT: Information Age Publishing.

Barnett, W. S. (2008). *Preschool education and its lasting effects: Research and policy implications.* Boulder, CO, and Tempe, AZ: Education and the Public Interest Center & Education Policy Research Unit.

Barnett, W. S., Epstein, D., Friedman, A., Stevenson Boyd, J., & Hustedt, J. (2008). *The state of preschool 2008.* New Brunswick, NJ: National Institute for Early Education Research.

Barnett, W. S., & Yarosz, D. J. (2007). Who goes to preschool and why does it matter? *National Institute for Early Education Research Policy Brief 15.* New Brunswick, NJ: National Institute for Early Education Research.

Barnett, W. S., Yarosz, D. J., Thomas, J., Jung, K., & Blanco, D. (2007). Two-way and monolingual English immersion in preschool education: An experimental comparison. *Early Childhood Research Quarterly, 22*(3), 277–293.

Baruth, L. G., & Manning, L. (1992). *Multicultural education of children and adolescents.* Needham Heights, MA: Allyn & Bacon.

Belle, D. (1990). Poverty and women's mental health. *American Psychologist, 45*(3), 385–389.

Benard, B. (1994). *Fostering resiliency in kids: Protective factors in the family, school, and community.* San Francisco, CA: WestEd.

Benard, B. (2004). *Resiliency: What we have learned*. San Francisco, CA: WestEd.

Bennett, L., Jr. (1966). *Before the Mayflower*. Baltimore: Penguin Books.

Bernhard, J. K., Cummins, J., Campoy, F. I., Ada, A. F., Winsler, A., & Bleiker, C. (2006). Identity texts and literacy development among preschool English language learners: Enhancing learning opportunities for children at risk for learning disabilities. *Teachers College Record, 108* (11), 2380–2405.

Bettler, R., & Burns, B. (2003). *Enhancing parental involvement through goal-based interventions*. Cambridge, MA: Harvard Family Research Project. Retrieved January 2009 from http://www.hfrp.org/publications-resources/publications-series/family-involvement-research-digests/enhancing-parental-involvement-through-goal-based-interventions

Bialystok, E. (2001). Metalinguistic aspects of bilingual processing. *Annual Review of Applied Linguistics, 21,* 169–181.

Bialystok, E. (2002). Acquisition of literacy in bilingual children: A framework for research. *Language Learning, 52* (1), 159–199.

Bowman, B. T., Donovan, S., & Burns, S. (2001). *Eager to learn: Educating our preschoolers*. Washington DC: National Academies Press.

Boyd, J., Barnett, W. S., Bedrova, E., Leong, D. J., Gomby, D., Robin, K. B., et al. (2005). *Promoting children's social and emotional development through preschool*. New Brunswick, NJ: National Institute for Early Education Research.

Boyd-Franklin, N. (2003). *Black families in therapy: Understanding the African American experience* (2nd ed.). New York: Guilford Press.

Brand, D. (1987, August 31). The new whiz kids. *Time,* (pp. 42–46, 51).

Brooks-Gunn, J., Brown, B., Duncan, G., & Moore, K. A. (1995). Child development in the context of family and community resources: An agenda for national data collection. *Integrating federal statistics on children: Report of a workshop* (pp. 27–97). Washington, DC: National Academy of Sciences.

Brooks-Gunn, J., & Duncan, G. (1997). The effects of poverty on children. *The Future of Children, 7* (2), 55–71. Retrieved April 2003 from http://www.futureofchildren.org/usr_doc/vol7no2ART4.pdf

Brooks-Gunn, J. Han, W., & Waldfogel, J. (2002). Maternal employment and child cognitive outcomes in the first three years of life: The NICHD Study of Early Child Care. *Child Development, 73,* 1052–1072.

Brooks-Gunn, J., Rouse, C., & McLanahan, S. (2007). Racial and ethnic gaps in school readiness. In R. C. Pianta, M. J. Cox, & K. Snow (Eds.), *School readiness and the transition to kindergarten* (pp. 283–306). Baltimore: Paul H. Brookes.

Bulcraft, R., Carmody, D., & Bulcraft, K. (1996). Patterns of paternal independence given to adolescents: Variations by race, age, and gender of child. *Journal of Marriage and the Family, 58* (4), 866–883.

Burchinal, M. R., Ramey, S. L., Reid, M. K., & Jaccard, J. (1995). Early child care experiences and their association with family and child characteristics during middle childhood. *Early Childhood Research Quarterly, 10,* 33–61.

Calderon, M., Gonzalez, R., & Lazarin, M. (2004). *State of Hispanic America, 2004*. Washington, DC: National Council of La Raza.

Cambio de Colores. (2007). *Latinos in Missouri: Gateway to a new community. Proceedings of the 2004 annual conference including selected papers from 2003*. University of Missouri Extension in cooperation with the Cambio Center. Columbia: University of Missouri – Columbia, March 2007.

Capps, R., Fix, M., & Reardon-Anderson, J. (2003). *Children of immigrants show slight reduction in poverty, hardship* (Working Paper). Washington, DC: Urban Institute.

Capps, R., Fix, M., Ost, J., Reardon-Anderson, J., & Passel, J. (2004). *The health and well-being of young children of immigrants*. New York: Urban Institute.

Castro, D. C., Gillanders, C., Machado-Casas, M., & Buysse, V. (2006). *Nuestros Niños Early Language and Literacy Program*. Chapel Hill: The University of North Carolina, FPG Child Development Institute.

Chan, S., & Lee, E. (2004). Families with Asian roots. In E. Lynch & M. Hanson (Eds.), *Developing cross-cultural competence: Working with young children and their families* (3rd ed., pp. 219–298). Baltimore: Paul H. Brookes.

Chang, F., Crawford, G., Early, D., Bryant, D., Howes, C., et al. (2007). Spanish speaking children's social and language development in pre-kindergarten classrooms. *Early Education and Development, 18,* 243–269.

Chau, M., & Douglas-Hall, A. (2007, September). *Low income children in the United States: National and state trend data, 1996–2006.* New York: National Center for Children in Poverty, Columbia University, Mailman School of Public Health.

Chiappe, P., & Siegel, L. S. (1999). Phonological awareness and reading acquisition in English- and Punjabi-speaking Canadian children. *Journal of Educational Psychology, 91* (1), 20–28.

Children Now. (2005). *California Report Card, 2005.* Oakland, CA: Author.

Compton-Lilly, C., & Comber, B. (2003). *Reading families: The literate lives of urban children.* New York: Teachers College Press.

Copple, C., & Bredekamp, S. (Eds.). (2009). *Developmentally appropriate practice in early childhood programs.* Washington, DC: National Association for the Education of Young Children.

Crosnoe, R. (2004). Double disadvantage or signs of resilience: The elementary school contexts of children from Mexican immigrant families. *American Educational Research Journal, 42,* 269–303.

Crosnoe, R., & Lopez-Gonzalez, L. (2005). Immigration from Mexico, school composition, and adolescent functioning. *Sociological Perspective, 48,* 1–24.

Cummins, J. (1994). Knowledge, power and identity in teaching English as a second language. In F. Genesee (Ed.), *Educating second language children: The whole child, the whole curriculum, the whole community.* (pp. 33–58). Cambridge: Cambridge University Press.

Delgado-Gaitan, C. (2004). *Involving Latino families in schools: Raising school achievement through home-school partnerships.* Thousand Oaks, CA: Corwin Press.

Deming, D. (2008). *Early childhood intervention and life-cycle skill development: Evidence from Head Start.* Cambridge, MA: Harvard University. Downloaded November 2008 from http://client.norc.org/jole/SOLEweb/9257.pdf

Diaz, R. M., & Klinger, C. (1991). Towards an explanatory model of the interaction between bilingualism and cognitive development. In E. Bialystok (Ed.), *Language processing in bilingual children* (pp. 140–185). New York: Cambridge University Press.

Dinan, K. A. (2006). *Young children in immigrant families: The role of philanthropy—Sharing knowledge, creating services, and building supportive policies.* Report of a meeting, January 18–19, 2006. New York: National Center for Children in Poverty. Retrieved January 2009 from http://www.nccp.org/publications/pdf/text_661.pdf

Douglas-Hall, A., Koball, H., & Chau, M. (2006). *Basic facts about low-income children, birth to age 18.* New York: National Center for Children in Poverty, Columbia University Mailman School of Public Health.

Duncan, G., & Brooks-Gunn, J. (Eds.). (1997). *Consequences of growing up poor.* New York: Russell Sage Foundation.

Early, D. M., Barbarin, O., Bryant, D., Burchinal, M., Chang, F., Clifford, R., et al. (2005). *Pre-kindergarten in eleven states: NCEDL's Multi-State Study of Pre-Kindergarten & Study of State-Wide Early Education Programs (SWEEP).* Chapel Hill, NC: NCEDL.

Early, D. M., Bryant, D. M., Pianta, R. C., Clifford, R. M., Burchinal, M. R., Ritchie, S., et al. (2006). Are teachers' education, major, and credentials related to classroom quality and children's academic gains in pre-kindergarten? *Early Childhood Research Quarterly, 21,* 174–195.

Eccles, J., & Gootman, J. A. (Eds.). (2002). *Community programs to promote youth development.* Washington, DC: National Academies Press.

Education Commission of the States. (2006). *Emerging state policy trends in early childhood education: A review of governors' 2006 state of the state addresses.* Denver, CO: Author. Retrieved December 2008 from http://www.ecs.org/html/Document.asp?chouseid=6821

Education Trust. (2003a). *African American achievement in America.* Retrieved November 2008 from http://www2.edtrust.org/edtrust/product+catalog/main

Education Trust. (2003b). *Latino achievement in America.* Retrieved November 2008 from http://www2.edtrust.org/edtrust/product+catalog/main

Education Trust. (2006). *Yes we can: Telling truths and dispelling myths about race and education in America.* Washington DC: Author.

Epstein, A. (2009). *Me, you, us: Social-emotional learning in preschool.* Washington DC: National Association for the Education of Young Children.

Epstein, J., Sanders, M., Simon, B., Salinas, K. A., Jansorn, N., & Voorhis, F. (2002). *School, family, and community partnerships: Your handbook for action* (2nd ed.). Thousand Oaks, CA: Corwin Press.

Espinosa, L. (1995). Hispanic involvement in *early childhood programs.* Urbana, IL: Eric Clearinghouse on Elementary and Early Childhood Education. (ED382412.)

Espinosa, L. (1998). School involvement and Hispanic parents. *The Prevention Researcher, 5*(1), 5–8.

Espinosa, L. (2003). Preschool program quality: What it is and why it matters. *National Institute of Early Education Research Policy Brief, 1* (1), 1–12.

Espinosa, L. (2005). Curriculum and assessment considerations for young children from culturally, linguistically, and economically diverse backgrounds. *Psychology in the Schools, 42* (8), 837–854.

Espinosa, L. (2007a). English-language learners as they enter school. In R. Pianta & K. Snow (Eds.), *School readiness, early learning, and the transition to school* (pp. 175–196). Baltimore: Paul H. Brookes.

Espinosa, L. (2007b). The social, cultural, and linguistic components of school readiness in young Latino children. In L. M. Beaulieu (Ed.), *The social-emotional development of young children from diverse backgrounds* (pp. 37–52). Baltimore: National Black Child Development Institute Press.

Espinosa, L. (2008a). *Challenging common myths about young English language learners.* Foundation for Child Development Policy Brief No. Eight. Available online at http://www.fcd-us .org/resources/resources_show.htm? doc_id= 669789

Espinosa, L. (2008b). *Assessing young English language learners for developmental outcomes.* Commissioned paper for the National Academies of Science Committee on Child Assessment and Outcomes. Washington, DC: National Academies Press.

Espinosa, L. (2008c). Early literacy for English language learners. In A. DeBruin-Parecki (Ed.), *Effective early literacy practice: Here's how, here's* why (pp. 71–86). Baltimore: Brookes Publishing.

Espinosa, L., Castro, D. C., Crawford, G., & Gillanders, C. (2007, May 15). *Early school success for English language learners: A review of evidence-based instructional practices for PreK to Grade three.* Paper presented at the First School Symposium, Early School Success: Equity and Access for Diverse Learners. Chapel Hill, NC.

Espinosa, L., & Lopez, M. (2007). *Assessment considerations for young English language learners across different levels of accountability.* Paper written for the National Early Childhood Accountability Task Force. Available online at http://www.pewtrusts.org/our_work.aspx? category=102

Espinosa, L., Laffey, J., & Whittaker, T. (2006a). *Language minority children analysis: Focus on technology use.* Final report to Center for Research on Evaluation, Standards and Student Testing/National Center for Educational Testing.

Espinosa, L., Laffey, J., & Whittaker, T. (2006b). Technology in the home and the achievement of young children: Findings from the Early Childhood Longitudinal Study (ECLS-K). *Early Education & Development, 17* (3), 421–441.

Espinosa, L. M., & Burns, M. S. (2003). Early literacy for young children and English-language learners. In C. Howes (Ed.), *Teaching 4- to 8-tear-olds: Literacy, math, multiculturalism, and classroom community* (pp. 47–69). Baltimore: Paul H. Brookes.

Espinosa, L. M., & Laffey, J. M. (2003). Urban primary teacher perceptions of children with challenging behaviors. *Journal of Children & Poverty, 9* (2), 23–44.

Espinosa, L., & Lesar, S. (1993). Family focus for school success: An early intervention program in Redwood City. *Thrust for Educational Leadership, 23,* 12–15.

Felsman, J. K. (1989). Risk and resiliency in childhood: The lives of street children. In T. Dugan & R. Coles (Eds.), *The child in our times* (pp. 56–80). New York: Bruner/Mazel.

Fields, J. (2003). Children's living arrangements and characteristics: March 2002. *Current Population Reports,* Series P20-547. Washington, DC: U.S. Bureau of the Census.

Fitzgerald, J. (1995a). English-as-a-second-language reading instruction in the United States: A research review. *Journal of Reading Behavior, 27* (2), 115–152.

Fitzgerald, J. (1995b). English-as-a-second-language learners' cognitive reading processes: A review of research in the United States. *Review of Educational Research, 65* (2), 145–190.

Fraser, M. W. (Ed.). (2004). *Risk and resilience in childhood.* Washington DC: NASW Press.

Fuligni, A. J., Tseng, V., & Lam, M. (1999). Attitudes toward family obligations among American adolescents with Asian, Latin American, and European backgrounds. *Child Development, 70,* 1028–1044.

Fuller, B. (2005). *Mapping the availability of center-based care in Latino communities.* Paper presented at the technical work group meeting of the National Task Force on Early Childhood Education for Hispanics, Tempe, AZ.

Galinsky, E. (2006). *The economic benefits of high-quality early childhood programs: What makes the difference?* Washington DC: The Committee for Economic Development with Funding from the A. L. Mailman Foundation.

Gandara, P., Rumberger, R., Maxwell-Jolly, J., & Callahan, R. (2003). *English learners in California schools: Unequal resources, unequal outcomes.* Retrieved May 2008 from the Educational Policy Analysis Archives Web site, http://epaa.asu.edu/epaa/v11n36/

Garcia, E. E. (1991). Caring for infants in a bilingual child care setting. *Journal of Educational Issues of Language Minority Students, 9,* 1–10.

Garcia, E. E. (2003). *Student cultural diversity: Understanding and meeting the challenge.* Boston: Houghton Mifflin.

Garcia, E. E. (2005). *Teaching and learning in two languages: Bilingualism and schooling in the United States.* New York: Teachers College Press.

Garcia, E. E., & Jensen, B. (2007). Helping young Hispanic learners. *Educational Leadership, 64* (6), 34–39.

Garcia, G. N. (2000). *Lessons from research: What is the length of time it takes limited English proficient students to acquire English and succeed in an all-English classroom?* (Issue Brief No. 5). Washington, DC: National Clearinghouse for Bilingual Education.

Garmezy, N. (1974). The study of competence in children at risk for severe psychopathology. In E. J. Anthony (Ed.), *The child in his family, Vol. 3: Children at psychiatric risk* (pp. 77–98). New York: John Wiley & Sons.

Garmezy, N. (1991). Resiliency and vulnerability to adverse developmental outcomes associated with poverty. *American Behavioral Scientist, 34* (4), 416–430.

Garmezy, N., & Rutter, M. (1983). *Stress, coping and development in children.* New York: McGraw-Hill.

Gee, J. P. (2001). A sociocultural perspective on early literacy development. In S. B. Neuman & D. K. Dickinson (Ed.), *Handbook of early literacy research* (pp. 30-42). New York: Guilford Press.

Genesee, E., Paradis, J., & Crago, M. B. (2004). *Dual language development and disorders: A handbook on bilingualism and second language learning.* Baltimore: Paul H. Brookes.

Goffin, S., & Lombardi, J. (1989). *Speaking out: Early childhood advocacy.* Washington, DC: National Association for the Education of Young Children.

Golan, S., Spiker, D., & Sumi, C. (2005). *Family support services promote school readiness.* Cambridge, MA: Harvard Family Research Project. Retrieved January 2009 from http://www.hfrp.org/publications-resources/browse-our-publications/family-support-services-promote-school-readiness

Goldenberg, C. (2006, July 26). Improving achievement for English-learners. *Education Week.*

Gonzalez, N. E., Moll, L., & Amanti, K. (2005). *Funds of knowledge: Theorizing practices in households, communities, and classrooms.* Mahwah, NJ: Lawrence Erlbaum Associates.

Gormley, W. T., Gayer, T., Phillips, D., & Dawson, B. (2005). The effects of universal pre-K on cognitive development. *Developmental Psychology, 41,* 872–884.

Hale, J. (1983). Black children: Their roots, culture and learning styles. In O. N. Saracho & B. Spodek (Eds.), *Understanding the multicultural* experience in early childhood education (pp. 17–34). Washington, DC: National Association for the Education of Young Children.

Hale, J. (2001). *Learning while black: Creating educational excellence for African American children*. Baltimore: The Johns Hopkins University Press.

Hall, E. T. (1977). *Beyond culture*. Garden City, NY: Anchor Press.

Halverson, C. F., & Waldrup, M. P. (1974). Relations between preschool barrier behaviors and early school measures of coping, imagination and verbal development. *Developmental Psychology, 10,* 716–720.

Hart, B., & Risley, T. R. (1995). *Meaningful differences in the everyday experience of young American children*. Baltimore: Paul H. Brookes.

Hart, B., & Risley, T. R. (1999). *The social world of children learning to talk*. Baltimore: Paul H. Brookes.

Harwood, R. L., Miller, J. G., & Irizarry, N. L. (1995). *Culture and attachment: Perception of the child in context*. New York: Guilford Press.

Heckman, J. J., & Masterov, D. V. (2007). *The productivity argument for investing in young children* (Working Paper No. 13016). Cambridge, MA: National Bureau of Economic Research. Retrieved September 2008 from http://www.nber.org/papers/w13016.pdf

Hernandez, D. (2006). [Unpublished tables on the 0–8 population in the 2000 Census]. National Task Force on Early Childhood Education for Hispanics: Tempe, AZ.

Hernandez, D. J. (2004). Demographic change and the life circumstances of immigrant families. *The Future of Children, 14* (2). Los Altos, CA: David and Lucille Packard Foundation.

Holzer, H. J., Schanzenbach, D. W., Duncan, G. J., & Ludwig, J. (2007). *The economic costs of poverty in the United States: Subsequent effects of children growing up poor* (Discussion Paper No. 1327-07). Madison, WI: Institute for Research on Poverty.

Huang, G. (1997). *Beyond culture: Communicating with Asian Pacific Islander American children and families*. New York: Teachers College Press, Columbia University.

Illinois Facilities Fund. (2003, June). *We need more day care centers*. Chicago, IL: Author.

Issacs, J. (2008). *The impacts of early childhood programs* (Brookings Center on Children and Families Research Brief No. 1). Retrieved December 2008 from www.brookings.edu/ccf

Kagan, S. L., Kauerz, K., & Tarrant, K. (2007). *The early care and education teaching workforce at the Folcrum: An agenda for reform*. New York: Teachers College Press.

Karoly, L. A., Ghosh-Dastidar, B., Zellman, G., Perlman, M., & Fernyhough, L. (2008). *Prepared to learn: The nature and quality of early care and education for preschool-age children in California*. Technical Report by the Rand Corporation 539. Retrieved from http://www.rand.org/pubs/technical_reports/TR539/

Kieff, J. (2008). *Informed advocacy in early childhood care and education: Making a difference for young children and families*. Upper Saddle River, NJ: Prentice Hall.

Klein, L., & Knitzer, J. (2006). *Effective preschool curricula and teaching strategies. Pathways to early school success* (Issue Brief No. 2). New York: National Center for Children in Poverty, Columbia University.

Knight, G. P., Virdin, L. M., & Rossa, M. (1994). Socialization and family correlates of mental health outcomes among Hispanic and Anglo American children: Considerations of cross-ethnic scalar equivalence. *Child Development, 65,* 212–224.

Knudsen, E. I., Heckman, J. J., Cameron, J. L., & Shonkoff, J. P. (2006). Economic, neurobiological, and behavioral perspectives on building America's future workforce. *Proceedings of the National Academy of Sciences, 103* (27), 10155–10162.

Korenman, S., Miller, J., & Sjaastad, J. (1994). *Long-term poverty and child development in the United States: Results from the NLSY* (Discussion Paper No. 1044-94). New York: Institute for Research on Poverty. Krashen, S., & Terrell, T. (1983). *The natural approach: Language acquisition in the classroom*. Englewood Cliffs, NJ: Prentice Hall.

Kuhl, P. K. (2004). Early language acquisition: Cracking the speech code. *Nature Reviews Neuroscience, 5* (11), 831–843.

Kuhl, P. (2007, January). The bilingual brain (Filmed Interview). *NBC Nightly News with Brian Williams.*

Kuhl, P., Tsao, F.-M., & Liu, H. (2003). Foreign-language experience in infancy: Effects of short-term exposure and social interaction on phonetic learning. *Proceedings of the National Academy of Sciences, 100* (15), 9096–9101. Available online at http://cat.inist.fr/?aModele=afficheN&cpsidt=150 04162

Lally, R., Lurie-Hurvitz, L., & Cohen, J. (2006). Good health, strong families, and positive early learning experiences: Promoting better public policies for America's infants and toddlers. *Zero to Three, 26* (6), 6–10.

Leafstedt, J. M., & Gerber, M. M. (2005). Crossover of phonological processing skills: A study of Spanish-speaking students in two instructional settings. *Remedial and Special Education, 26* (4), 226–235.

Lee, V., & Burkam, D. (2002). *Inequality at the starting gate: Social background differences in achievement as children begin school.* Washington, DC: Economic Policy Institute.

Logan, S. L. (2001). *The Black family: Strengths, self-help and positive change.* Boulder, CO: Westview Press.

Lonigan, C. J. (2006). Development, assessment, and promotion of preliteracy skills. *Early Education and Development, 17* (1), 91–114.

Lopez, E. S., & de Cos, P. L. (2004). *Preschool and childcare enrollment in California* (No. CRB99009). Sacramento: California Research Bureau.

Lopez, G. R. (2001). The values of hard work: Lessons on parent involvement from an (im)migrant household. *Harvard Educational Review, 71* (3), 416–437.

Lopez, L. M., & Greenfield, D. B. (2004). Cross-language transfer of phonological skills of Hispanic Head Start children. *Bilingual Research Journal, 28* (1), 1–18.

Lopez, M., Barrueco, S., & Miles, J. (2006). *Latino infants and their families: A national perspective of protective and risk factors for development* (Unpublished document). Laytonsville, MD: National Center for Latino Children & Family Research.

Lynch, E. W., & Hanson, M. J. (Eds.). (2004). *Developing cross-cultural competence: Working with young children and their families* (3rd ed.). Baltimore: Paul H. Brookes.

Magnuson, K., Ruhm, C., & Walgfogel, J. (2007). Does prekindergarten improve school preparation and performance? *Economics of Education Review, 26,* 33–51.

Manning, L. (2005). *Diversity within: A typology of first-generation Mexican parenting* (Dissertation Proposal). Columbia, MO: University of Missouri—Columbia.

Masten, A. (2001). Ordinary magic: Resilience processes in development. *American Psychologist, 56* (3), 227–238.

Mayer, S. E. (1997). *What money can't buy: Family income and children's life chances.* Cambridge, MA: Harvard University Press.

McCartney, K., & Weiss, H. (2007). Data for a democracy: The evolving role of evaluation in policy and program development. In J. L. Aber, S. J. Bishop-Josef, S. M. Jones, K. T. McLearn, & D. A. Phillips (Eds.), *Child development and social policy: Knowledge for action* (pp. 59–76). Washington, DC: American Psychological Association.

McCartney, M., Belsky, J., Vandell, D. L., Burchinal, M., Clarke-Stewart, K. A., McCartney, K., et al. (2007). Are there long-term effects of early child care? *Child Development, 78* (2), 681–701.

McClelland, M. M., Morrison, F. J., & Holmes, D. L. (2000). Children at risk for early academic problems: The role of learning-related social skills. *Early Childhood Research Quarterly, 15* (3), 307–329.

McLaughlin, B. (1984). Are immersion programs the answer for bilingual education in the United States? *Bilingual Review, 11* (1), 3–11.

McLaughlin, B. (1995). Fostering second language development in young children: Principles and practices (NCRCDSLL Educational Practice Reports, EPR14). Berkeley, CA: Center for Research on Education, Diversity & Excellence.

McLaughlin, B., Blanchard, A., & Osanai, Y. (1995). *Assessing language development in bilingual preschool children.* Washington DC: National Clearinghouse for English Language Acquisition.

McLoyd, V. C., Hill, N. E., & Dodge, K. (Eds.). (2005). *African American family life: Ecological and cultural diversity.* New York: Guilford Press.

McNaughton, S. (2005). Considering culture in research-based interventions to support literacy. In D. Dickinson & S. Neuman (Eds.), *Handbook of early literacy research* (Vol. 2, pp. 229–242). New York: Guilford Press.

Meisels, S. (2007). No easy answers: Accountability in early childhood. In R. C. Pianta, M. J. Cox, & K. Snow (Eds.), *School readiness, early learning and the transition to kindergarten* (pp. 31–48). Baltimore: Paul H. Brookes.

Moll, L. C., Armanti, C., Neff, D., & Gonzalez, N. (1992). Funds of knowledge for teaching: Using a qualitative approach to connect homes and classrooms. *Theory into Practice, 31* (2), 132–141.

National Association for the Education of Young Children (NAEYC) and the National Association of Early Childhood Specialists in State Departments of Education (NAECS/SDE). (2003). *Early childhood curriculum, assessment, and program evaluation: Building an effective, accountable system in programs for children birth through age 8.* A Joint Position Statement of the NAEYC and NAECS/SDE. Washington DC: NAEYC.

National Early Literacy Panel. (2007, March). *Findings from the National Early Literacy Panel: Providing a focus for early language and literacy development.* PowerPoint presentation to the 10th Annual National Conference on Family Literacy, Orlando, FL.

National Early Literacy Panel. (2008). National Early Literacy Panel research and dissemination to support early literacy development in young children. Retrieved April 2008 from http://www.nifl.gov/nifl/NELP/NELPreport.html

National Center for Children in Poverty. (1999). *Poverty and brain development in early childhood.* Retrieved September 2008 from http://www.nccp.org/publications/pub_398.html

National Center for Children in Poverty. (2007). *Who are America's poor children?* Retrieved September 2008 from http://www.nccp.org/publications/pub_787.html

National Center for Education Statistics. (2003). *Status and trends in the education of Hispanics.* Washington DC: U.S. Department of Education, National Center for Education Statistics.

National Commission on Teaching and America's Future. (2007). *Building a 21st century U.S. education system.* Retrieved January 2009 from http://www.nctaf.org/strategies/assure/index.htm

National Institute of Child Health and Human Development Early Child Care Research Network. (2005). Duration and developmental timing of poverty and children's cognitive and social development from birth through third grade. *Child Development, 76* (4), 795–810.

National Scientific Council on the Developing Child at Harvard University. (2007a). *A science-based framework for early childhood policy: Using evidence to improve outcomes in learning, behavior, and health for vulnerable children.* Retrieved January 2009 from http://www.developingchild.harvard.edu

National Scientific Council on the Developing Child at Harvard University. (2007b). *The science of early childhood development: Closing the gap between what we know and what we do.* Retrieved January 2009 from http://www.developingchild.harvard.edu

National Scientific Council on the Developing Child at Harvard University. (2007c). *The timing and quality of early experiences combine to shape brain architecture* (Working Paper No. 5). Retrieved January 2009 from http://www.developingchild.harvard.edu

National Scientific Council on the Developing Child at Harvard University. (2008). *Mental health problems in early childhood can impair learning and behavior for life* (Working Paper No. 6). Retrieved January 2009 from http://www.developingchild.net

National Task Force on Early Education for Hispanics. (2007). *Para nuestros niños: Expanding and improving early education for Hispanics.* Tempe, AZ: Author. Available online at http://www.ecehispanic.org/index.html

Nissani, H. (1990). Early childhood programs for language minority children (FOCUS: Occasional Papers in Bilingual Education, No. 2). Washington, DC: National Clearinghouse for Bilingual Education.

Office of Head Start. (2008). *Dual language learning: What does it take?* (Head Start Dual Language Report). Washington, DC: Administration for Children and Families.

Okagaki, L., & Frensch, P. (1998). Parenting and children's school achievement: A multiethnic perspective. *American Educational Research Journal, 35* (1), 123–144.

Oller, D. K., & Eilers, R. (2002). *Language and literacy in bilingual children*. Tonawanda, NY: Multilingual Matters, Ltd.

Paratore, J. R. (2005). Family and community involvement in children's reading and literacy development: A response to Steven Sheldon and Joyce Epstein. In J. Flood & P. Anders (Eds.), *Closing the achievement gap in urban schools: Setting the research agenda* (pp. 139–150). Newark, DE: International Reading Association.

Partnership for America's Economic Security. (2008). Web site. Retrieved September 2008 from http://www.partnershipforsuccess.org

Pearson, B. Z. (2001). Narrative competence in bilingual children in Miami. In D. K. Oller & R. E. Eilers (Eds.), *Language and literacy development in bilingual children* (pp. 135–174). Clevedon, UK: Multilingual Matters.

Pease-Alvarez, L., & Hakuta, K. (1992). Enriching our views of bilingualism and bilingual education. *Educational Researcher, 21* (2), 4–6.

Penn State Newsletter *LIVE*. (2009, May). Available online at http://www.hbg.psu.edu/

Phillips, M., Brooks-Gunn, J., Duncan, G. J., Klebanov, P., & Crane, J. (1998). Family background, parenting practices, and the Black-White test score gap. In C. Jencks & M. Phillips (Eds.), *The Black-White test score gap* (pp. 103–145). Washington, DC: Brookings Institution.

Pianta, R. C., Cox, M., & Snow, K. (Eds.). (2007). *School readiness and the transition to kindergarten in the era of accountability*. Baltimore: Paul H. Brookes.

Portes, A., & Rumbaut, R. G. (2001). *Ethnicities: Children of immigrants in America*. Berkeley: University of California Press.

Portes, P., & Zady, M. (2002). Self-esteem in the adaptation of Spanish-speaking adolescents: The role of immigration, family conflict, and depression. *Hispanic Journal of Behavioral Sciences, 24* (3), 296–318.

Pungello, E. P., Campbell, F. A., & Barnett, S. W. (2006). *Poverty and early childhood education.*

Center for Poverty, Work and Opportunity Policy Brief Series. Retrieved November 2008 from http://www.law.unc.edu/centers/poverty/publications.aspx

Ramey, S., & Ramey, C. (1989). Developmental psychology and mental retardation: Integrating scientific principles with treatment practices. *American Psychologist, 44,* 409–415.

Raver, C. C. (2002). *Emotions matter: Making the case for the role of young children's emotional development for early school readiness*. Ann Arbor, MI: Society for Research in Child Development.

Raver, C. C., & Zigler, E. F. (1997). Social competence: An untapped dimension in evaluating Head Start's success. *Early Childhood Research Quarterly, 12,* 363–385.

Ray, A., Bowman, B., & Robbins, J. (2006). Preparing early childhood teachers to successfully educate all children (Foundation for Child Development Policy Report, September 2006). Retrieved November 2008 from http://www.fcd-us.org/resources/resources_show.htm?doc_id=463599

Reese, L., Goldenberg, C., & Saunders, W. (2006). Variations in reading achievement among Spanish-speaking children in different language programs: Explanations and confounds. *Elementary School Journal, 106* (4), 363–385.

Reuschenberg, E., & Buriel, R. (1989). Mexican American family functioning and acculturation: A family systems perspective. *Hispanic Journal of Behavioral Sciences, 11* (3), 232–244.

Reyes, I., & Moll, L. C. (2006). Bilingualism and Latinos. In I. Stavans (Ed.), *Encyclopedia Latina: History, culture, and society in the United States* (pp. 181–185). New York: Grolier.

Reynolds, A. J., Temple, J. A., Robertson, D. L., & Mann, E. A. (2001). Long-term effects of an early childhood intervention on educational achievement and juvenile arrest: A 15-year follow-up of low-income children in public schools. *Journal of the American Medical Association, 285* (18), 2330–2346.

Rhymer, R. (1993). *Genie: An abused child's flight from silence*. New York: HarperCollins.

Rist, R. (2000). Student social class and teacher expectations: The self-fulfilling prophesy in ghetto education. *Harvard Education Review, 40,* 266–301. (Reprinted from R. Rist, 1970, Student social class and teacher expectations: The self-fulfilling prophecy in ghetto education. *Harvard Education Review, 40,* 72–73.)

Rodriguez, J. L., Duran, D., Diaz, R. M., & Espinosa, L. (1995). The impact of bilingual preschool education on the language development of Spanish-speaking children. *Early Childhood Research Quarterly, 10,* 475–490.

Rothenberg, A. (Ed.). (1995). *Understanding and working with parents and children from rural Mexico.* Menlo Park, CA: The CHC Center for Child and Family Development Press.

Rumberger, R., & Anguiano, A. (2004). *Understanding and addressing the California Latino achievement gap in early elementary school* (Working Paper 2004-01). University of California, Santa Barbara.

Rumberger, R., & Larson, K. (1998). Toward explaining differences in educational achievement among Mexican American language-minority students. *Sociology of Education, 71,* 69–93.

Rutter, M. (1984). Resilient children. *Psychology Today,* pp. 57–65.

Rutter, M. (1993). Resilience: Some conceptual considerations. *Journal of Adolescent Health, 14,* 626–631.

Sadowski, M. (2006). *Core knowledge for PK-3 teaching: Ten components of effective instruction* (Foundation for Child Development Policy Brief No. 5). Retrieved November 2008 from http://www.fcdus.org/resources/resources_show.htm?doc_id=462123

Schweinhart, L. J., Montie, J., Xiang, Z., Barnett, W. S., Belfield, C. R., & Nores, M. (2005). *Lifetime effects: The High Scope Perry Preschool Study through age 40.* Yipsilanti, MI: High Scope Press.

Segal, J. (1986). *Winning life's toughest battles: Roots of human resilience.* New York: McGraw-Hill.

Shade, B., & Edwards, P. (1987). Ecological correlates of the educative style of Afro-American children. *Journal of Negro Education, 56*(1), 88–99.

Shonkoff, J. P., & Phillips, D. A. (Eds.). (2000). *From neurons to neighborhoods. The science of early childhood development.* Washington, DC: National Academies Press.

Slavin, R. E., & Cheung, A. (2005). A synthesis of research on language of reading instruction for English language learners. *Review of Education Research, 75* (2), 247–281.

Smith, B. (2008). *Linking social development and behavior to school readiness* (Handout 4.3: Leadership Strategies from The Center on the Social and Emotional Foundations for Early Learning, University of Illinois at Urbana-Champaign). Downloaded October 2008 from www.challengingbehavior.org/do/resources/documents/rph_social_dev_school_rediness.pdf

Snow, C. E., Burns, M. S., & Griffin, P. (Eds.). (1998). *Preventing reading difficulties in young children.* Washington, DC: National Academies Press.

Stebbens, H., & Langford, B. (2006). *Guide to calculating the cost of quality of early care and education.* Washington DC: The Finance Project. Retrieved September 2008 from http://www.financeproject.org/publications/costguide.pdf

Stewart, J. C. (1996). *1001 things everyone should know about African American history.* New York: Doubleday.

Storti, C. (2001). *The art of crossing cultures.* London, UK: Nicholas Brealey Publishing.

Tabors, P., & Snow, C. (1994). English as a second language in preschools. In F. Genesee (Ed.), *Educating second language children: The whole child, the whole curriculum, the whole community* (pp. 103–125). New York: Cambridge University Press.

Tabors, P. O. (1997/2008). *One child, two languages: A guide for preschool educators of children learning English as a second language.* Baltimore: Brookes Publishing.

U.S. Census Bureau. (2003, January 21). Census Bureau releases population estimates by age, sex, race and Hispanic origin. *United States Department of Commerce News.* Washington, DC: U.S. Department of Commerce.

U.S. Census Bureau. (2004). Hispanics and Asian Americans increasing faster than overall population. *United States Department of Commerce News.* Retrieved June 14, 2004, from http://

www.census.gov/Press-Release/www/releases/archives/race/001839.html

U.S. Department of Health and Human Services. (2003). *State-funded pre-kindergarten: What the evidence shows*. Retrieved June 2008 from http://aspe.hhs.gov/hsp/state-funded-pre-k/index.htm

U.S. Department of Health and Human Services, Administration for Children and Families. (2009). *Head Start impact study and follow-up, 2000–2009*. Retrieved January 2009 from http://www.acf.hhs.gov/programs/opre/hs/impact_study/index.html

U.S. Department of Health and Human Services, Administration for Children and Families, Head Start Bureau. (2001). *Linguistic diversity and early literacy: Serving culturally diverse families in Early Head Start* (Technical Paper No. 5). Washington, DC: Early Head Start National Resource Center @ ZERO TO THREE.

Valdés, G. (1996). *Con Respeto: Bridging the distances between culturally diverse families and schools. An ethnographic portrait*. New York: Teachers College Press.

Valencia, R. (2000). Inequalities and the schooling of minority students in Texas. *Hispanic Journal of Behavioral Sciences, 22,* 445–459.

Walsh, F. (2003). *Spiritual resources in family therapy*. New York: Guilford Publications.

Wang, M. C., & Walberg, H. J. (Eds.). (2004). *Building academic success on social and emotional learning: What does the research say?* (pp. 1–22). New York: Teachers College Press, Columbia University.

Wentzel, K., & Asher, S. (1995). The academic lives of neglected, rejected, popular, and controversial children. *Child Development, 66,* 754–763.

Werner, E. (1990). Protective factors and individual resilience. In S. Meisels & J. Shonkoff (Eds.), *Handbook of early childhood intervention* (pp. 97–116). New York: Cambridge University.

Werner, E., & Smith, R. (1989). *Vulnerable but invincible: A longitudinal study of resilient children and youth*. New York: Adams, Bannister, and Cox.

Werner, E. E., & Smith, R. S. (1992). *Overcoming the odds: High-risk children from birth to adulthood*. Ithaca, NY: Cornell University Press.

Werner, E., & Smith, R. (2001). *Journeys from childhood to midlife. Risk, resilience, and recovery*. Ithaca, NY: Cornell University Press.

Whitehurst, R. (2004). *Dialogic reading: An effective way to read to preschoolers*. Available online at http://www.readingrockets.org/article.php?id=431

Willis, W. (2004). Families with African American roots. In E. L. Lynch & M. J. Hanson (Eds.), *Developing cross-cultural competence: Working with young children and their families* (3rd ed., pp. 141–178). Baltimore: Paul H. Brookes.

Winsler, A., Diaz, R. M., Espinosa, L., & Rodriguez, J. L. (1999). When learning a second language does not mean losing the first: Bilingual language development in low-income, Spanish-speaking children attending bilingual preschool. *Child Development, 70* (2), 349–362.

Wong Fillmore, L. (1976). *The second time around: Cognitive and social strategies in second language acquisition*. Unpublished doctoral dissertation, Stanford University, Palo Alto, CA.

Wong Fillmore, L. (1979). Individual differences in second-language acquisition. In C. J. Fillmore, D. Kempler, & W. Wang (Eds.), *Individual differences in language ability and language behavior* (pp. 203–228). New York: Academic Press.

Wong Fillmore, L. (1991). When learning a second language means losing the first. *Early Childhood Research Quarterly, 6,* 323–346.

Wong Fillmore, L. (2000, Autumn). Loss of family languages: Should education be concerned? *Theory into Practice*, 203–210.

Yao, E. L. (1988). Working effectively with Asian immigrant families. *Phi Deltan Kappan, 70,* 223–225.

Yeh, S. S. (2003). An evaluation of two approaches for teaching phonemic awareness to children in Head Start. *Early Childhood Research Quarterly, 18* (4), 513–529.

Yeh, S. S., & Connell, D. B. (2008). Effects of rhyming, vocabulary and phonemic awareness instruction on phoneme awareness. *Journal of Research in Reading, 31* (2), 243–256.

Zahn-Waxler, C., Duggal, S., & Gruber, R. (2002). Parental psychopathology. In M. H. Bornstein (Ed.), *Handbook of parenting* (2nd ed., pp. 3–43). Mahwah, NJ: Erlbaum.

Zigler, E. (2005). Head Start policy: Comments on Currie, and Hustedt and Barnett. In R. E. Tremblay, R. G. Barr, & R. De. V. Peters (Eds.), *Encyclopedia on early childhood development* [online]. Montreal, Quebec: Centre of Excellence for Early Childhood Development, pp. 1–5. Retrieved January 2009 from http://www.enfant-encyclopedie.com/Pages/PDF/ZiglerANGxp .pdf

Zins, J., Bloodworth, M., Weissberg, R., & Walberg, H. (2004). The scientific base linking social and emotional learning to school success.

Zins, J., Weissberg, R., Wang, M., & Walberg, H. (Eds.). (2004). *Building academic success on social and emotional learning: What does the research say?* (pp. 1–22). New York: Teachers College Press, Columbia University.

INDEX

If you like this book,
check out these titles available from NAEYC!

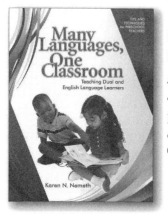

Many Languages, One Classroom: Teaching Dual and English Language Learners

Karen N. Nemeth

This resource includes adaptable strategies to help English language learners during reading, science, dramatic and outdoor play, blocks, and circle time. *From Gryphon House.* **Order #378**

Anti-Bias Education for Young Children and Ourselves

Louise Derman-Sparks & Julie Olsen Edwards

The eagerly awaited successor to the influential *Anti-Bias Curriculum!* Become a skilled anti-bias teacher with this volume's practical guidance to confronting and eliminating barriers of prejudice, misinformation, and bias; most importantly, find tips for helping staff and children respect each other, themselves, and all people. **Order #254**

Diversity in Early Care and Education: Honoring Differences
(5th ed.)

Janet Gonzalez-Mena

This book explores the rich diversity encountered in early childhood programs. An important resource for early childhood professionals who want to forge positive relationships within today's diverse society. *From McGraw-Hill.* **Order #2011**

Also available as a set

Practice in Building Bridges

Intisar Shareef & Janet Gonzalez-Mena

Written especially for NAEYC, this collection of activities, discussion topics, stories, and ideas for journaling is designed as a companion resource for those using Janet Gonzalez-Mena's book *Diversity in Early Care and Education.* **Order #2012**